An Introduction to Creative Writing

Dr. Zarina Deshmukh

Copyright © <Published Year> <Author Name>

Made with ❤ on the Notion Press Platform

www.notionpress.com

Contents

CONTENTS

Preface

I've been writing since I was in high school. I have been doing it for decades now—quietly, persistently, and often without an audience. Like many writers, I had a manuscript or two safely tucked away in folders labelled "final draft," which are anything but final. Life happened. Confidence wavered. And deadlines never helped. So, my books stayed on the shelf—unpublished and unread. I wrote my first book a decade ago, but like most first loves, it never quite made it out into the world until recently.

It wasn't until I began teaching Creative Writing at the university that I realised something important. Students don't necessarily need a step-by-step manual telling them how to write creatively. In fact, I found that they often already had stories inside them, voices waiting to be heard. What they really needed—before the writing exercises and story arcs—was a basic understanding of *what* creative writing truly is.

This book was born out of that need.

When I looked through the available books in our university library, I found they were all written by foreign authors. Many were excellent, yes—but often far removed from the context and clarity my students were looking for. They were either too academic or too abstract. And sometimes, the language itself became a barrier.

So, I decided to write a book—not on *how* to write creatively, but on *what* creative writing is. This book aims to be an introduction, not a lecture. I've kept the language simple, the tone accessible, and the content structured in a way that welcomes not only Creative Writing students, but anyone—teachers, readers, curious minds—who wants to understand what creative writing involves.

Throughout the chapters, I've included references to various literary works, not to overwhelm the reader, but to do two things. First, to help students relate to the kind of writing they might already have encountered in their syllabus or outside it. And second, to offer a gentle nudge toward reading more. If you haven't read the books mentioned, you now have a reading list you didn't ask for—but may end up loving. Think of it as your creative starter kit.

At the end of the book, I've also included one of my personal blog posts titled *Biopics of Writers That Will Make You Want to Write*. It's a light, inspiring read that brings together films based on the lives of writers—stories of eccentric habits, relentless passion, and the occasional bout of glorious writer's block. If you ever find yourself stuck or unmotivated, watching how some of the greatest writers stumbled, persevered, and eventually found their voice might just help you find yours.

Creative writing can be taught, yes—but only to those who bring a spark of motivation and a willingness to explore their own voice. It isn't about finding the "right" way to write. It's about being honest, curious, and open to discovering how words can reflect the world you live in, the worlds you imagine, and the ones you long to understand.

This book won't turn you into a bestselling author overnight (if it does, please write to me), but I hope it makes you pause, think, and pick up your pen—or keyboard—with a little more confidence than before.

Welcome to creative writing.

You can write to me at zarina.deshmukh@gmail.com

Warmly,
Dr. Zarina Deshmukh

Acknowledgments

First and foremost, I would like to thank the Almighty—for the brilliant decision to bring me into existence. Had I not been born, I wouldn't have had to go through the relentless inner monologue, sleepless nights, existential dread, and the typing marathon that led to this book. So, thank you, Universe. Great call.

To my parents—thank you for the gift of intelligent genes and for always reminding me that I could do more, be more, and never quite hit "enough." Without that gentle (and sometimes not-so-gentle) push, I wouldn't have felt the intense need to prove something by publishing *not just* my first academic book, but my second book overall. Look at me now—validation in print.

To my dear family and friends—thank you for your zero contribution. The way you all managed to carry on with your lives, unaffected and blissfully detached from this entire writing process, truly inspired me. Your silence, lack of interference, and occasional "Oh, you're still working on that?" kept me grounded.

To my colleagues—your endless emails, cryptic meeting agendas, and refusal to reply to things on time have toughened me up in ways no self-help book ever could. You've truly prepared me for the emotional warfare that is the publishing industry.

To my students—thank you for your wild questions, unconventional creativity, and occasional inability to read instructions. You made me realize that most of the creative writing books out there are just... not it. And only *I* could save you from the vague and verbose wasteland of what's already out there. You didn't ask for it, but you're welcome anyway.

And finally, to myself— because when the dust settled, and everyone else went to bed, *I* was still here—editing, proofreading, obsessing over fonts, and crying over formatting issues that refused to obey logic. Publishing is hard. Self-publishing is a full-time hobby disguised as a nightmare. But this is *creative writing*, so of course the process had to be extra dramatic.

Part I:

Foundations of Creative Writing

Chapter 1

Understanding Creative Writing

Humans are the only beings who are blessed with the ability to think. Thinking leads them to put their opinion and thoughts forward. Writing is one of the most profound forms of expression available to humankind. It enables them to communicate their thoughts, emotions and idea across generations. Spoken words may fade with time, written words preserve the experiences of the writer long after he is gone. Even in his absence his stories, philosophies and experiences are shared with the wide world for centuries.

Writing allows people to reflect, question and express like no other medium of expression. A single sentence can spark a change, bring in a revolution or challenge the status quo. Writing allows people to find a sanctuary within and explore their inner worlds. Its therapeutic and gives a sense of catharsis to put words to paper (or to keyboard) making sense of the complex emotions, self-discovery and identifying personal growth.

Writing connects us to the world. The inner turmoil or the conflicts that finds its way to the paper when shared with the world, it gives an assurance that the whole world is out there which relates with everything the writer has written, creating a shared understanding and empathy. A divided world by borders, culture, and perspectives; written words remind us of our common humanity.

In the digital age, the power of writing is perhaps more relevant than ever. As information becomes increasingly abundant and easily accessible, the need for clear, compelling writing is crucial. Whether it's crafting blog posts, writing academic papers, or penning social media captions, the ability to communicate effectively through writing is a skill that enhances every aspect of life.

Creative writing is not confined to a rigid definition. It's an expansive, dynamic art that allows us to express thoughts, emotions, and ideas in ways that break through the boundaries of everyday communication. Think about the moments when you're lost in a novel, enchanted by a poem, or moved by a character's journey in a play.

Creative writing offers a medium to experience and create those moments. Unlike academic or technical writing, which focuses on facts and analysis, creative writing exists in a fluid space where the imagination takes the lead, guiding us through stories, poems, dramas, or reflections that speak to the human experience. Creative writing allows you to explore worlds, characters, and situations that might not exist in reality, but can feel real through words.

1.1 Understanding the Basics

At its core, creative writing is about crafting something entirely new from your imagination. It could be a short story, a novel, a poem, or even a screenplay. It is the act of building worlds, whether they are fictional or grounded in reality. Imagine the vast, immersive universe of Gabriel García Márquez's *One Hundred Years of Solitude*, a world where magical realism breathes life into every sentence, drawing readers into a narrative that feels both fantastical and deeply real. Or think about Chimamanda Ngozi Adichie's *Americanah*, a novel that paints a touching picture of identity and displacement, capturing the essence of human experience in a way that resonates universally—works that build whole worlds and characters that feel vividly real, even though they spring from fiction.

The beauty of creative writing lies in its originality and the emotional depth it conveys. You are not merely conveying information or instructing the reader; you are inviting them into a space crafted from your imagination, where they can experience a new reality or perspective. This freedom to create is what makes creative writing both exciting and challenging.

Creative writing isn't about presenting dry facts or adhering to stringent structures. Instead, it's about letting your creativity flow and allowing your unique voice to shape your narrative. It's the process of turning thoughts and feelings into words that not only entertain but also engage and inspire.

1.2 Different Forms of Creative Writing

Creative writing comes in many flavours, can take many forms, and each offers a unique way of telling a story or sharing ideas.

Fiction

This is where stories born from the imagination come to life. It can be based on real-life experiences, but the events and characters are created by the writer. Fiction includes short stories, novellas, and novels. Within fiction, there are many genres, such as fantasy, science fiction, romance, thriller, and historical fiction, each with its own rules and conventions. Whether it's J.K. Rowling's wizarding world in *Harry Potter* or the complex narratives of characters in a short story, fiction gives us a space to escape and dream. Through fiction, you can create entire universes, populate them with characters who face extraordinary challenges, and plots that push the boundaries of reality.

Poetry

Poetry is a form of creative writing that uses rhythm, sound, and imagery to express feelings and ideas. Poems can be short or long, simple or complex, but they often play with language in ways that are different from prose. Poetry allows for more emotional and symbolic expression, using meter, rhyme, and free verse to convey the writer's thoughts. In just a few lines poetry can evoke deep emotions, painting vivid pictures with sound, rhythm, and imagery. Poetry often captures moments and feelings that are too complicated for prose, allowing readers to experience the essence of a thought or emotion in a condensed form.

Drama

Drama involves writing scripts for plays. It focuses on dialogue and actions between characters and is meant to be performed in front of an audience. Through drama, writers can create conflict, build tension, and explore deep emotional themes. Whether it's the tragic complexities of

Hamlet or the raw emotion of *A Streetcar Named Desire*, writing for the stage or screen engages audiences in intense emotional experiences. Drama is unique in that it translates written words into performances, where actors embody the characters and bring the script's emotional and narrative arcs to life.

Creative Non-fiction

Unlike fiction, creative non-fiction is based on real events, but it uses storytelling techniques found in fiction to make the writing engaging. Memoirs, personal essays, and travel writing are examples of creative non-fiction. It combines factual accuracy with the writer's personal voice, making it both informative and reflective. Take an example of Elizabeth Gilbert's travel fiction *Eat, Pray, Love* where she uses narrative depth and emotional resonance while remaining rooted in personal experience.

Personal Journals or Diaries

While personal journals are often written for private reflection, they can also serve as a form of creative writing. Journals allow writers to explore their inner thoughts, emotions, and experiences, often leading to deep personal insights or inspiring future works of fiction or poetry. The example is in Anne Frank's *The Diary of a Young Girl*, which offers intimate insights into the human spirit. Journals and diaries provide a space for raw, unfiltered expression, capturing the writer's innermost thoughts and feelings.

1.3 The Purpose of Creative Writing

Why do writers write? There is no singular answer, creative writing serves many purposes, and each writer may have their own reasons for engaging in it. However, some common purposes may include:

- **Expression:** One of the most important functions of creative writing is self-expression. Through creative writing, you can share your personal experiences, thoughts, emotions, and worldviews. It allows you to communicate complex ideas and emotions in a way that might not be possible through other forms of writing. Toni Morrison's *Beloved* is a powerful example of writing that explores the trauma of slavery while delving into themes of love and memory. Through creative writing, we can articulate feelings and ideas that might otherwise remain unspoken, offering readers a window into the complexities of human experience.

- **Entertainment:** It can also be used to entertain. Whether through gripping stories, funny anecdotes, or dramatic plays, creative writing provides readers with an escape from the real world. Great writing can captivate and entertain, as seen in the timeless wit of Jane Austen's *Pride and Prejudice* or the imaginative worlds of Neil Gaiman's *Neverwhere*. Entertainment through creative writing provides an escape from the mundane, offering readers a chance to immerse themselves in new worlds and experiences.

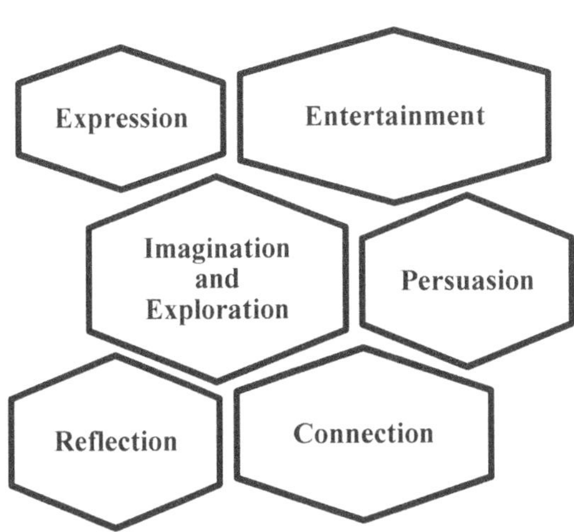

- **Persuasion:** It can serve the purpose of persuasion as well, using storytelling or emotive language to influence the reader's thoughts, opinions, or actions. Whether it's through a compelling narrative, an emotional poem, or a thought-provoking play, creative writing can subtly or overtly advocate for social change, inspire new perspectives, or challenge existing beliefs. This allows writers to communicate powerful messages and potentially shape the reader's worldview.

- **Imagination and Exploration:** It offers a space to explore different ideas, scenarios, and worlds. You can experiment with "what if" questions—what if people could fly? What if history took a different path? This type of writing allows for imaginative exploration, letting writers push the boundaries of reality. Consider *Brave New World* by Aldous Huxley or *1984* by

George Orwell, where they take readers on journeys through alternate realities that reflect and question our own world. Imagination allows writers to explore hypothetical scenarios, and offer new perspectives on familiar issues.

- **Connection:** Many writers use creative writing to connect with others. Stories, poems, and plays can reflect universal themes like love, loss, hope, and fear, helping readers relate to the work on a deeper level. Through writing, writers often find ways to touch the hearts of readers and make them feel understood. As Paulo Coelho puts it, "I write for people with the same soul as mine." (Paulo Coelho official blog)

- **Reflection:** It is a tool for reflection and introspection. Writers often explore personal experiences, beliefs, and emotions through their writing, which can lead to greater understanding of themselves and the world around them. Books that explore the theme of wars shows the emotional weight of war, giving readers a lens through which to understand courage, fear, and loss. Creative writing allows us to process and make sense of our experiences, offering both the writer and the reader a deeper understanding of the human condition.

1.4 The Elements of Creative Writing

Creative writing is more than just putting words on paper; it involves carefully crafting different elements to create a cohesive and engaging piece.

Plot: The plot is the sequence of events in a story. It includes the beginning (introduction of characters and setting), the middle (the conflict or main problem), and the end (the resolution of the conflict). A well-crafted plot propels the story forward, as seen in Margaret Atwood's *The Handmaid's Tale*, where tension and suspense keep readers engaged. The plot is the skeleton of your story, providing structure and direction. It's what keeps the reader turning pages, eager to find out what happens next. In Harper Lee's *To Kill a Mockingbird*, themes of racial injustice, moral growth, and empathy are woven throughout the plot, as the characters confront prejudice and the complexities of human nature. These themes challenge readers to reflect on morality and social inequality. In Mary Shelley's *Frankenstein*, themes of creation, isolation, and the consequences of playing God drive the narrative. Shelley's exploration of scientific ambition and its ethical implications raises questions about humanity, responsibility, and the boundaries of knowledge.

Setting: The setting is the time and place where the story happens. Whether it's a real location or an imaginary world, the setting helps build the atmosphere of the story. A well-described setting immerses readers in the world of the narrative. Take for example, the foggy streets of Charles Dickens' *Great Expectations* or the windswept moors in Emily Brontë's *Wuthering Heights* that create atmospheres that enhance the narrative and captivates the readers. In Ernest Hemingway's *The Old Man and the Sea*, the vast, open sea serves as both a physical and metaphorical setting that represents the themes of struggle, perseverance, and the human condition in the face of nature. Setting isn't just a backdrop; it's an integral part of the story that can influence the mood and tone.

Theme: The theme is the central idea or message of the story. Themes in creative writing explore deeper meanings, such as love, identity, morality, or justice. Writers often use themes to make their work more meaningful and thought-provoking. In *Moby Dick*, Herman Melville explores obsession, fate, and the human struggle. In George Orwell's *1984*, Orwell brings themes of totalitarianism, surveillance, and the loss of individual freedom, illustrating the dangers of oppressive regimes and the manipulation of truth. These themes provoke reflection on the nature of power and control in society. In F. Scott Fitzgerald's *The Great Gatsby*, themes of the American Dream, social class, and the illusion of happiness are central. Through Gatsby's pursuit of wealth and status, Fitzgerald critiques the idea of the American Dream and the hollowness of material success. Themes provide depth and resonance, giving readers something to ponder long after they've finished the story.

Character: Characters are the people or beings in your story. In fiction and drama, characters are essential because they drive the plot forward. Writers must create well-rounded, believable characters with distinct personalities, motivations, and flaws. In The Great Gatsby, Scott Fitzgerald has brought the character of Gatsby to life that made him unforgettable through his depth and growth of his character in the novel. The character of Will Traynor in Jojo Moyes' *Me Before You* is complex illustrating the characteristics through his choices as he grapples with his physical limitations and emotional struggles, making him both relatable and thought-provoking. Similarly, in Gillian Flynn's *Gone Girl*, the characters of Nick and Amy Dunne stand out due to their psychological depth and intricate manipulation, with Amy's cunning and Nick's flaws creating a dynamic that keeps readers questioning their motives and loyalties, exploring the themes of deception, the manipulation of truth, and the darker side of marriage. Well-developed characters drive the narrative, offering readers someone to relate to, root for, or even despise; like the character of Iago from Shakespeare's *Othello*.

Dialogue: Dialogue is the spoken conversation between characters. Good dialogue sounds natural and helps reveal the characters' personalities and emotions. It also helps to move the plot forward by showing interactions between characters. Mark Twain's *The Adventures of Huckleberry Finn* showcases authentic speech patterns, bringing characters to life through their words. Ernest Hemingway in his *The Sun Also Rises*, uses the minimalistic and direct dialogue between characters that reflect their emotional detachment and disillusionment, capturing the post-war generation's inner turmoil and moving the story forward through subtle exchanges. While in Jane Austen's *Pride and Prejudice*, the witty and sharp dialogue between Elizabeth Bennet and Mr. Darcy reveals their evolving relationship. Their exchanges, filled with tension, humour, and eventual understanding, not only highlight their distinct personalities but also drive the romantic and social dynamics of the story. Effective dialogue can convey personality, build relationships, and move the story forward.

Tone and Style: The tone of a piece of creative writing refers to the attitude or emotion conveyed by the writer. It could be serious, humorous, sarcastic, or melancholic, depending on the writer's intention. Style refers to the unique voice of the writer—the way they use words, sentence structure, and literary devices to create a distinct feel to the writing. The tone in Arundhati Roy's *The God of Small Things* is melancholic and reflective, as it explores themes of forbidden love, family secrets, and societal constraints in a moving and evocative manner. While talking about style, look at Salman Rushdie's *Midnight's Children*; Rushdie's style is rich and exuberant, blending magical realism with historical and political commentary, creating a vibrant and intricate narrative that reflects the complexities of post-colonial India. The tone of a piece sets its emotional register, whether it's the sharp wit of Oscar Wilde's *The Importance of Being Earnest* or the lyrical beauty of Virginia Woolf's *To the Lighthouse*. Tone and style are what give a piece of writing its unique flavour and emotional impact.

Imagery and Description: In creative writing, the use of vivid imagery and detailed descriptions can bring a story to life. Writers often use descriptive language to appeal to the reader's senses, helping them to visualize, hear, feel, or even smell what's happening in the story. Rich imagery can transport readers to a different time, place, or mood. F. Scott Fitzgerald's *The Great Gatsby* is renowned for its lush descriptions that create a vivid sense of time and place. Imagery and description help readers visualize and feel the world of the story, making it come alive in their minds.

1.5 The Creative Writing Process

Creative writing is a process that often takes time and practice. The writing process in creative writing refers to the series of steps that writers follow to develop, craft, and refine their work. While the process can vary from writer to writer, it typically consists of several key stages that help shape a creative piece, whether it's fiction, poetry, scripts, or non-fiction.

Brainstorming: In creative writing, brainstorming is a process used to generate ideas and explore possibilities for your writing project. It involves free and open thinking about various concepts, themes, characters, and plot points without immediately judging or filtering them. The goal is to unleash creativity and uncover new, innovative ideas that can be developed into a story, poem, or other forms of writing. Idea generation is a key aspect of brainstorming. Writers generate a wide range of ideas, whether for a story plot, character traits, settings, or themes. This can be done through listing, mind-mapping, or free-writing.

Brainstorming allows writers to explore different directions their writing could take. This might include experimenting with various plot twists, character motivations, or settings. During brainstorming, writers are encouraged to think without limitations or self-censorship. This helps in generating unique and creative ideas that might not emerge during more structured planning. Writers often use tools like prompts, images, random word generators, or story dice to stimulate their imagination and explore different ideas. The brainstorming process is essential in the early stages of writing, helping to lay the foundation for more structured planning and development later on.

Planning: Planning is an essential step in the process of creative writing that helps transform an idea into a structured narrative. While some writers prefer to leap into writing without a set plan, others find that having a roadmap offers clarity and direction, helping them avoid the potential pitfalls of writer's block or meandering plotlines. Planning involves making decisions about your story's structure, character development, and the sequence of events, creating a foundation upon which your narrative can unfold.

When it comes to planning, outlining is a common technique used by many writers. A well-organised outline allows you to chart the key events and conflicts in your story, giving you a clear path from beginning to end. Whether you're writing a short story, novel, or screenplay, this step ensures that your ideas don't stray from the central narrative. Outlining can be as simple as listing major plot points or as detailed as creating scene-by-scene breakdowns. Writers like J.K. Rowling have famously shared detailed outlines, showing how planning helps weave together complex plots.

Character development is another critical aspect of planning. Before you start writing, it can be helpful to think deeply about your characters—their backstory, desires, conflicts, and arcs. Well-planned characters often lead to more engaging and believable narratives, as their motivations and choices feel consistent and thought out. Mapping out how your characters will evolve throughout the story adds layers of depth to your work.

Even for writers who prefer a more organic approach to storytelling, having a basic framework or understanding of key moments can guide the creative process. Ultimately, planning in creative writing is about finding the right balance between structure and spontaneity, ensuring that your ideas can grow while maintaining coherence and focus.

Drafting: Drafting is the phase in creative writing where your ideas take shape on the page. It's the moment when you begin to translate thoughts, emotions, and images into words. The primary goal during drafting is not perfection but progress—getting your ideas down without the pressure of them being polished or complete.

At this stage, it's important to embrace the idea of the "bad first draft," a concept famously championed by writer Anne Lamott. The focus is on writing without inhibition, allowing yourself the freedom to make mistakes, explore different angles, and follow your creative impulses. Perfection can come later during the revision process. For now, it's about capturing the essence of your narrative, no matter how rough or disorganised it might feel.

Drafting can be messy, with half-formed ideas, awkward sentences, or inconsistencies in character or plot. That's perfectly okay. What matters is momentum—moving forward and getting the words out. By releasing the need for perfection, you free your creativity to explore new possibilities and directions. Remember, the first draft is only the beginning, and every great piece of writing starts somewhere.

Revising: Revising is a critical step in the creative writing process where you refine and reshape your initial draft. Once the first draft is complete, revising allows you to look at your work with fresh eyes, focusing on improving the structure, clarity, and overall flow of the writing. This stage is about making the narrative stronger, ensuring it communicates your intended message effectively.

During revision, you may notice areas that need more detail or sections that feel repetitive or unnecessary. You might rework scenes, clarify dialogue, or adjust pacing to keep the reader engaged. It's not just about fixing surface-level errors but about deepening the story's impact.

Sometimes, revision involves significant changes—rearranging chapters, rewriting dialogue, or even cutting entire sections that don't serve the overall narrative.

Revision also offers an opportunity to enhance the emotional and thematic layers of the piece, sharpening the tone or voice. By revisiting your work with a critical perspective, you allow your story, poem, or play to evolve, shaping it into a more cohesive and compelling piece of writing. It's through revision that your ideas become clearer, your language more precise, and your storytelling more effective.

Editing and Proofreading: Editing and proofreading are the final stages of the creative writing process, where you refine the technical aspects of your work. After revising for structure and content, editing focuses on polishing the language to ensure clarity, consistency, and style. In this phase, you correct grammar, punctuation, and sentence structure, making sure that the writing flows smoothly and is easy to understand. It's about improving readability and making sure every word serves its purpose.

Editing also involves eliminating redundancy, tightening sentences, and enhancing word choice to ensure the writing aligns with the tone and style you've developed. You may also fine-tune transitions between paragraphs and check for overall coherence. Attention to detail is key here, as the goal is to ensure that the piece reads fluidly without distractions.

Proofreading is the final pass through your work, a meticulous check for any remaining typos, spelling errors, or formatting issues. It's the last opportunity to ensure the text is clean and professional before it's considered finished. Proofreading requires a sharp eye and patience, as even small mistakes can detract from the reader's experience. Together, editing and proofreading help elevate your writing, making it polished and ready for presentation.

Sharing and Feedback: Once you feel satisfied with your draft after revising, editing, and proofreading, getting outside perspectives can provide valuable insights. Sharing your writing with trusted friends, family, or a writing group opens up opportunities for constructive criticism that can reveal aspects of your work you might not have considered.

Feedback allows you to see your story, poem, or essay through the eyes of others, helping to identify areas where clarity may be lacking, where a scene or character might need more development, or where pacing and tone could improve. Often, writers become so close to their work that it's hard to spot potential weaknesses or inconsistencies. Hearing from others can bring a fresh perspective, highlighting parts that resonate well and those that might need refinement.

However, it's important to approach feedback with an open mind. Not all suggestions will align with your vision, and that's okay. The goal is to use feedback to make your writing stronger, while staying true to your own voice. In the end, sharing your work and embracing the feedback process enhances your growth as a writer and sharpens your ability to self-edit effectively.

1.6 The Role of Inspiration in Creative Writing

Inspiration plays a vital role in creative writing, serving as the spark that ignites a writer's imagination and motivates them to bring their thoughts and emotions to life through words. Without inspiration, the creative process can feel stagnant and lifeless, but with it, writing takes on a vibrant and dynamic energy. For many writers, inspiration is a deeply personal experience that can stem from various sources—nature, art, personal experiences, or even simple, everyday moments.
Inspiration can be said be driving the creative writing process. It can arrive unexpectedly, sometimes when least expected, or it can be actively sought out by those who make a habit of looking for it in their surroundings. Often, it's that moment of sudden clarity or the overwhelming urge to capture a fleeting thought that motivates a writer to sit down and start crafting.

For many writers, inspiration begins with observation. Emily Dickinson, for example, found a great deal of her inspiration in nature. Her poems, rich in detail, reflect her deep connection with the natural world and her ability to draw creative ideas from her environment. Observing the world around you, noticing small details, and being attuned to the sensory experiences of everyday life can offer countless opportunities for inspiration. A single image—a bird perched on a windowsill, the sound of rain against the pavement, or a flower bending under the weight of dew—can be enough to trigger a wave of creativity that leads to a poem, a story, or a meaningful scene in a novel. Being inspired by an ordinary sight or sound allows writers to infuse their work with authenticity and relatability, making it resonate with readers on a deeper level.

Drawing from Personal Experiences

Personal experiences are another powerful source of inspiration for many writers. Life's events—both big and small—can have a profound effect on how writers approach their craft. Whether it's love, heartbreak, joy, or sorrow, these emotions provide the foundation upon which a writer can build a narrative or convey a message that feels raw and genuine.

The practice of keeping a journal is one method many writers use to capture and document moments of inspiration drawn from their lives. Journals serve as a repository for ideas, thoughts, emotions, and observations. Journaling encourages writers to regularly engage with their thoughts and the world around them, making a deeper connection to their inner creative voice.

Personal experience also allows writers to inject emotional depth into their writing. When a writer channels their own emotions into a piece of fiction or poetry, it can add a layer of authenticity and vulnerability that resonates with readers. Writers who have faced significant life challenges, such as grief or loss, often find that these experiences provide a rich source of inspiration for stories that deal with similar themes. Writing, in this sense, becomes both an outlet for emotional expression and a way to connect with others who may have experienced similar struggles.

The Role of Nature and the World Around Us

Nature has long been a source of inspiration for writers throughout history. The natural world, with its ever-changing beauty and unpredictability, offers endless opportunities for creative inspiration. From the tranquil imagery of a sunset to the ferocity of a storm, nature's contrasts often mirror the emotional landscapes explored in creative writing. Many writers draw parallels between the external world and the inner emotional journey of their characters, using natural elements as symbols or metaphors to enrich their storytelling by paying close attention to the environment.

Art, Music, and Other Creative Works

Beyond personal experiences and the natural world, inspiration for creative writing can also come from other forms of art. Writers often find that exposure to visual art, music, film, and even other literature can spark new ideas and encourage them to approach their writing from a fresh perspective. Inspiration is not bound by medium; sometimes, the emotions evoked by a painting or the mood set by a piece of music can provide the catalyst for a new creative work.

The interconnectedness of the arts allows writers to find inspiration in unexpected places. A visit to an art gallery, listening to a favourite album, or watching a thought-provoking film can trigger ideas that evolve into fully realized pieces of creative writing. By engaging with other creative works, writers expose themselves to different ways of thinking, seeing, and interpreting the world, all of which can fuel their own creativity.

Writing Prompt

Close your eyes and think of a time when something in your environment unexpectedly caught your attention. It could be as simple as the way sunlight through the leaves, a conversation you overheard in a café, or an old photograph. Picture that moment in detail. Now, write a scene, a short story, or poem that brings this moment to life. Focus on sensory details—what did you see, hear, smell, or feel? Write at least 500 words without restrictions.

The Importance of Nurturing Inspiration

While inspiration may be the starting point of the creative process, it's up to the writer to nurture it into something more. A single spark of inspiration is just the beginning—writing requires dedication, discipline, and effort to turn that initial idea into a fully formed piece. Writers must be willing to explore and expand upon their ideas, often through multiple drafts, revisions, and reworking of material. Nurturing inspiration means staying committed to the process of writing, even when the initial excitement wanes. By continuing to write, even when inspiration feels distant, writers develop the resilience needed to bring their creative visions to life. Inspiration is a powerful force, but it's the writer's perseverance and willingness to refine their craft that leads to truly exceptional creative writing.

1.7 Why Study Creative Writing?

Studying creative writing offers more than just the ability to tell stories. It is a way to develop your voice, explore new perspectives, and gain a deeper understanding of yourself and the world around you. Creative writing encourages personal growth, intellectual discovery, and reflection on human nature. This study goes beyond crafting sentences and plotlines—it helps you connect with emotions, engage with diverse viewpoints, and express ideas in ways that resonate with others. In this process, you not only become a better writer but also a more thoughtful and reflective individual.

Developing Your Unique Voice

One of the main reasons to study creative writing is to develop your own unique voice. Every writer has their own style, tone, and way of expressing ideas. Studying creative writing helps you discover this voice by providing opportunities to experiment with different writing forms, techniques, and genres. As you write more, you begin to understand what makes your writing stand out and what elements of your style are most effective in conveying your thoughts.

Take, for instance, the distinct voices of well-known authors like Zadie Smith, Chimamanda Ngozi Adichie, or Gabriel García Márquez.

These writers have developed unique ways of telling stories that reflect their cultural backgrounds, personal experiences, and worldviews. Through creative writing, you can also find your voice, allowing you to express yourself in ways that are true to who you are.

Enhancing Critical Thinking and Problem-Solving Skills

Creative writing requires you to think critically about every element of your story, whether it's character development, plot structure, or dialogue. As you study creative writing, you learn to ask questions like: What motivates this character? How does this event move the plot forward? Is the pacing of the story effective? These questions require a deep level of critical thinking, helping you develop analytical skills that are valuable not only in writing but also in other areas of life.

Problem-solving is another important skill you gain from studying creative writing. Writing a story often involves challenges, such as finding the right ending, resolving conflicts between characters, or maintaining a consistent tone throughout. By grappling with these challenges, you learn how to solve problems creatively, using your imagination to find solutions that make the story work. For example, in Salman Rushdie's novels, he often blends magical realism with historical events, a challenging task that requires careful thought about how to integrate fantastical elements with reality. By studying creative writing, you learn to tackle similar challenges in your own work, developing skills that can be applied in a wide range of contexts.

Exploring Different Perspectives

Creative writing allows you to step into other people's shoes and explore different perspectives. Whether you're writing from the viewpoint of a character who is vastly different from you or crafting a story set in a different time or place, creative writing pushes you to think outside your own experiences. This practice fosters empathy and broadens your understanding of the world.

Many writers have used creative writing to explore different cultures, histories, and identities. For instance, Jhumpa Lahiri's stories often deal with the immigrant experience, capturing the tension between different cultures and the complexities of identity. Similarly, Haruki Murakami's works explore the inner lives of characters who feel disconnected from society, reflecting broader themes of isolation and existential searching. By studying creative writing, you gain the tools to explore perspectives beyond your own. This practice not only improves your writing but also helps you engage more thoughtfully with the world around you.

Emotional Expression and Healing

Creative writing is a powerful tool for emotional expression. It allows you to explore your feelings and process emotions in a constructive way. Many people find that writing helps them make sense of difficult experiences or gain clarity on personal issues. Through writing, you can articulate emotions that might be hard to express in everyday conversation, making it a valuable outlet for emotional healing. Sylvia Plath's poetry often grapples with themes of mental health, depression, and personal struggle. Her writing gave her a way to express her feelings in a raw, honest form, and her work continues to resonate with readers who face similar challenges. In a similar way, studying creative writing can help you find a space to express emotions that might otherwise remain bottled up, providing a therapeutic outlet for self-expression.

Gaining a Deeper Appreciation for Storytelling

Storytelling is an essential part of the human experience. From ancient myths to modern novels, stories have always played a central role in how we understand ourselves and the world. By studying creative writing, you gain a deeper appreciation for the power of storytelling and the impact it can have on individuals and societies.

Writers like Toni Morrison, whose novels explore the complexities of race, history, and identity, demonstrate how stories can challenge societal norms, raise awareness about social issues, and inspire change. Through creative writing, you come to understand that storytelling is not just about entertainment—it is a way to convey deeper truths, connect with others, and spark dialogue. As you study creative writing, you also learn to appreciate the craftsmanship that goes into great storytelling.

You begin to notice the careful choices writers make in terms of language, structure, and character development.

Building Confidence in Self-Expression

Writing is a form of self-expression, and studying creative writing can help you build confidence in your ability to express your thoughts and ideas clearly and persuasively. Many people struggle with self-expression, especially when it comes to writing. However, as you practice and receive feedback in creative writing workshops or classes, you gain confidence in your abilities. Whether you are writing fiction, poetry, or personal essays, creative writing encourages you to share your voice with others. Over time, this practice can help you become more comfortable with expressing yourself in a range of settings, from personal conversations to professional communications.

Expanding Career Opportunities

While many people study creative writing for personal fulfilment, it can also open up a wide range of career opportunities. The skills you develop through creative writing—such as critical thinking, problem-solving, communication, and empathy—are valuable in many fields. Whether you pursue a career as a writer, editor, journalist, teacher, or content creator, creative writing provides a strong foundation for professional growth. Creative writing can lead to opportunities beyond publishing, including roles in media, marketing, education, and the arts.

A Path to Self-Discovery and Growth

Studying creative writing is not just about learning the mechanics of storytelling—it's about exploring your voice, understanding the power of narrative, and gaining new perspectives. It encourages self-discovery, emotional expression, and intellectual growth. Whether you want to become a published author, develop your writing skills, or simply explore new ways of thinking, creative writing offers a path to personal and professional enrichment. Through this study, you learn to articulate your thoughts with clarity, engage with different perspectives, and appreciate the transformative power of storytelling.

References

Atwood, Margaret. *The Handmaid's Tale*. McClelland & Stewart, 1985.

Austen, Jane. *Pride and Prejudice*. Salem Press, 1813.

Brontë, Emily. *Wuthering Heights*. Oxford University Press, 1847.

Flynn, Gillian. *Gone Girl*. Broadway Books, 2012.

Frank, Anne. *Diary of a Young Girl*. Penguin Publishers, 2018.

Gaiman, Neil. *Neverwhere : Author's Preferred Text*. William Morrow, 2021.

Gilbert, Elizabeth. *Eat, Pray, Love* . Riverhead Books, 2017.

Hemingway, Ernest. *The Old Man and the Sea*. Bloom's Literary Criticism, 1952.

https://paulocoelhoblog.com/author/paulo-coelho. "How I Write." *Paulo Coelho*, 16 Feb. 2012, paulocoelhoblog.com/2012/02/16/how-i-write/.

Huxley, Aldous. *Brave New World*. Bloom's Literary Criticism, 1932.

Melville, Herman. *Moby Dick*. 1851. Acclaim Books, 1997.

Morrison, Toni. *Beloved*. Vintage, 1987.

Moyes, Jojo. *Me before You*. Penguin Books, 2013.

Orwell, George. *1984*. 1949. Secker & Warburg, 1949.

Roy, Arundhati. *The God of Small Things*. 4Th Estate, 2017.

Shakespeare, William. *Hamlet*. 1603. American Scholar Publications, 1965.

Shelley, Mary. *Frankenstein*. Lackington, Hughes, Harding, Mavor & Jones, 1818.

Twain, Mark. *The Adventures of Huckleberry Finn*. 1884. Sirius, 1884.

Wilde, Oscar. *Importance of Being Earnest: And Other Plays*. Penguin, 1999.

Williams, Tennessee. *A Streetcar Named Desire*. Script City, 1995.

Chapter 2

The Importance of Research in Creative Writing

Research is a systematic investigation. It is a backbone of any writing. In creative writing, it is often hidden but it undeniably plays an essential role. It is the foundation upon which new ideas with engaging, believable, and insightful stories are built. Creative writing is highly dependent on imagination, research acts as its backbone. Research allows writers to create authentic settings, realistic characters, and accurate plots. It enhances the depth and credibility of their work. It is the lighthouse that guides the writers whether it is historical fiction, fantasy, or even contemporary novels. Research provides the facts and knowledge that bring writers' creative ideas to life.

As writer and teacher Eudora Welty said, *"Fiction depends for its life on place."* But beyond place, it also depends on the intricate realities that make up the worlds we imagine. As a writer begin to look for the information to shape their perspectives, what are the aspects to be looked at, how to find unbiased data and write authentic piece of fictional work. This chapter, will explore why research is crucial to creative writing, the types of sources available, and strategies for organizing your research effectively.

2.1 Why Research Matters in Creative Writing

At first glance, it may seem that research belongs more to academic or non-fiction writing, but it's just as vital in fiction. Why? Because while imagination lets us build new worlds, research ensures those worlds are consistent and believable. As Stephen King notes in On Writing, *"If you want to be a writer, you must do two things above all others: read a lot and write a lot.*" (King 145) But intertwined with that reading is research—an often invisible force that grounds our stories in reality, even when we're writing about dragons or dystopian futures.

Enhancing Authenticity and Credibility

Research gives your story authenticity. When you're writing about a historical period, location, or profession, getting the facts right is essential. When readers pick up your story, they're entering a world of your creation, but they want that world to feel real. Inaccuracy can pull them out of the narrative. Imagine writing a historical novel set in Victorian England but mixing up the details of fashion, speech, or even common technologies of the time. Readers will notice, and it will break the trust they've placed in your story. This is why research matters— whether you're depicting the life of a 19th-century factory worker or a modern astronaut, getting the details right lends your writing credibility.
If you're writing a novel set during World War II, understanding the historical context, political climate, and even the slang of that era will add layers of richness to your writing. Similarly, even in fantasy or science fiction, research can help you build logical and consistent worlds. Readers may suspend belief about dragons and magic, but they expect the internal logic of the world to hold up, which requires thoughtful research.

Take *All the Light We Cannot See* by Anthony Doerr as an example. The novel's beautifully detailed depiction of life during World War II is bolstered by extensive research into the time period, from the architecture of Saint-Malo to the intricacies of radio technology. The result is a work of fiction that feels real and grounded, despite being imaginative. Similarly, even when writing fantasy or science fiction, research is essential. In *A Game of Thrones*, George R.R. Martin builds a world full of dragons, magic, and ancient feuds, but the political dynamics and warfare are grounded in historical realities, inspired by events like the War of the Roses. This blend of imagination and research creates a world that readers can lose themselves in, while still feeling the pulse of authenticity.

Adding Depth to Characters and Plot

Research not only affects the setting but also plays a significant role in character development. Great characters are not born in a vacuum. They are shaped by their environments, professions, and experiences—all of which require research. By researching the backgrounds of your characters, you can create more complex, multidimensional personalities. Understanding a character's environment, experiences, and historical moment helps you shape their motivations, dialogue, and interactions in a way that is both believable and emotionally engaging.

For instance, if your protagonist is a lawyer, you'll need to understand legal terminology, the day-to-day life of legal professionals, and the ethical dilemmas they face. This knowledge will not only make your character more credible but also allow you to incorporate authentic conflicts and challenges into the plot. Consider the character of Atticus Finch in Harper Lee's *To Kill a Mockingbird*. His role as a lawyer, his views on justice, and his calm demeanour are intricately tied to the social, political, and legal realities of the 1930s American South. Without research into the racial tensions and legal frameworks of that era, his character wouldn't carry the same weight or significance. Or think about a novel where the protagonist is a surgeon. To make their actions, dialogues, and ethical dilemmas feel real, you would need to research medical procedures, terminology, and the lifestyle of a healthcare professional. This research ensures that the character's profession informs their motivations and conflicts, adding layers to both the character and the plot.

Supporting Thematic Depth

Research is also crucial when you're exploring larger themes in your work. If your story revolves around social issues, philosophical questions, or political conflicts, research allows you to handle these topics with sensitivity and accuracy. In doing so, you can provide new insights and perspectives to your readers. If you're writing about climate change, for example, immersing yourself in scientific studies and expert interviews will not only give your writing depth but will also allow you to engage meaningfully with the topic.

Margaret Atwood's *The Handmaid's Tale* is a powerful example of research supporting thematic exploration. Atwood used historical and contemporary events—like the oppression of women in various societies—as research to build the dystopian world of Gilead. This grounding in real-world history gives the novel its unsettling sense of plausibility, making its themes of power and control all the more impactful.

Inspiring New Ideas

Research isn't just a tool for filling in the blanks— sometimes, it can also be a source of inspiration. As writer Zadie Smith said, *"The very reason I write is so that I might not sleepwalk through my entire life."* As you gather information, you might stumble upon an interesting fact, an unusual event, or a historical figure that triggers new plotlines or character arcs.

When Hilary Mantel wrote *Wolf Hall*, she spent years researching the life of Thomas Cromwell. Through her research, Mantel uncovered details about Cromwell that allowed her to create a portrait of a man often seen as a villain in history. The richness of Cromwell's character and the intricacy of the historical backdrop all stem from Mantel's extensive research.

Writing Prompt

Research to Build a World
Choose a story idea that excites you, whether it's historical, contemporary, or fantastical. Now, pick one aspect of this world that requires research—this could be the setting, the time period, a specific profession, or even a cultural practice. Conduct research for about 30 minutes on that topic. Take notes on key facts, details, or ideas that stand out to you.
Task:
1. Write a 500-word scene from your story where the research you conducted plays a key role. Use your findings to add depth to your characters, plot, or setting.
2. Underline or highlight the details that stem directly from your research.
3. At the end of your scene, list at least three specific pieces of information you included from your research.

2.2 Types of Research Sources in Creative Writing

Research in creative writing comes from a variety of sources, each offering different perspectives and depths of information. Understanding how to use them effectively can greatly improve your writing. There are three main types of sources in creative writing research: primary sources, secondary sources, and tertiary sources. Primary sources, such as interviews, diaries, and firsthand accounts, bring an intimate level of detail, while secondary sources like books, articles, and documentaries provide context and analysis. Creative research can also extend to experiential methods, where sensory immersion and personal observation enrich the writer's connection to the subject. By effectively integrating these varied research tools, writers can craft richer, more informed stories that resonate with readers.

Primary Sources

Primary sources are first-hand accounts—diaries, letters, interviews, and eyewitness testimonies—that provide raw, personal insights into specific events or eras. They allow you to immerse yourself in the thoughts, feelings, and experiences of those who lived through the time you're writing about. For example, if you're writing a novel about the Great Depression, reading the diaries of individuals who lived through that era can give you a first-hand understanding of their struggles, emotions, and day-to-day experiences. These human insights are invaluable for creating believable and relatable characters. In addition, primary sources can help capture the language, customs, and societal norms of a particular period, adding depth to your narrative.

Secondary Sources

Secondary sources are one step removed from the actual event or experience. They analyse, interpret, or summarize primary sources. These include newspaper articles, biographies, documentaries, and academic papers. Secondary sources are useful for gaining a broader understanding of a topic and are often packed with factual information. While secondary sources may not provide the emotional depth of primary sources, they help establish the larger context of the story you're telling. They're essential for ensuring that your narrative feels cohesive and historically accurate, giving you a full grasp of the period or topic you're writing about. For instance, if your novel is set during the French Revolution, reading historical analysis will give you a broad understanding of the social and political forces at play. Biographies of key figures will also give you a clear understanding of the political and social climate, which can influence the plot and conflicts in your story.

Tertiary Sources

Tertiary sources are further removed from the original experience, often synthesizing and summarizing secondary sources. Examples include textbooks, encyclopedias, and reference books. While these are often starting points, they provide quick overviews of key topics. Tertiary sources can provide you with a basic overview of a subject, helping you understand key concepts before diving into more detailed research. For example, if you're writing a sci-fi novel involving space travel, *Astrophysics for People in a Hurry* by Neil deGrasse Tyson can provide a clear, accessible introduction to key astrophysics concepts, making it a useful starting point for your book. From there, you can explore more detailed or specialized texts to further enhance the science in your sci-fi novel.

2.3 Organising Your Research

When gathering research for a writing project, it's easy to become overwhelmed by the sheer volume of information. If your research isn't organised, you may find yourself wasting time searching for facts, losing track of key details, or feeling swamped by data. To avoid this, it's crucial to adopt an effective system to organise your research. A well-structured organisation system not only helps you maintain clarity but also allows you to quickly retrieve relevant information, cross-reference ideas, and ensure accuracy in your writing. By categorising notes, labelling sources, and maintaining clear files, you prevent confusion and maintain focus. There are different methods with which you can organise your research.

1. File or Binder System:

Some writers prefer a hands-on approach, using physical folders,

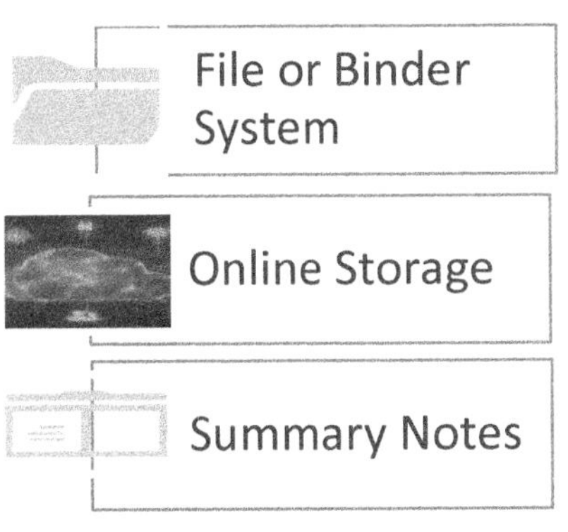

binders, and notebooks to organise their research. This system allows you to interact with your material in a tactile way, which can be especially helpful if you're the kind of person who enjoys working with hard copies or needs to see all of your information laid out in front of you. The hands-on nature of a physical system is advantageous for the writer as you may find that having physical papers to handle and organise helps you retain and understand the material better. Additionally, when it's laid out in front of you, it's easier to see patterns and connections between different pieces of information.

With a file or binder system, you can categorize your notes and research according to specific themes, characters, or plot points. This method is particularly useful for projects that require attention to detail, such as historical novels or biographies. For example, author Hilary Mantel, while working on her historical novel *Wolf Hall*, kept detailed files about Thomas Cromwell's world. She used a meticulously organised filing system to ensure that she had all the facts, dates, and references easily accessible. By grouping her research into different categories, she could quickly find specific information without having to sift through an overwhelming pile of notes.

2. Online Storage:

For those who prefer a more modern approach, digital tools offer an efficient way to organise research. Tools like Google Drive, Evernote, and Scrivener allow you to store all your research electronically. One of the biggest advantages of using digital storage is that it can handle large quantities of information in a flexible, accessible, and organised way.

Digital systems allow you to create folders, use tags, and easily search through your documents. If you're working on a complex project with multiple layers of research, such as a science fiction novel or a multi-part series, this method is incredibly helpful. You can categorize your research by topic, character, or timeline and then search for specific keywords when you need to find a particular fact or quote.

Google Drive, for example, allows you to store documents, images, and other types of media. Evernote offers tagging features and the ability to clip web pages directly into your research notebook, making it easy to gather information from different online sources. Scrivener is a tool specifically designed for writers, providing built-in templates and organisational tools to streamline both research and writing. An additional benefit of online storage is accessibility. As long as you have internet access, you can access your research from any device—whether it's a laptop, phone, or tablet; from anywhere. This makes it easier to work on the go or reference something when you're away from your desk.

With the advent of AI, it became easier. Tools like IKI.AI efficiently sorts through vast amounts of information, they save time and reduce overwhelm, allowing writers to focus on crafting compelling narratives. These tools can categorize sources, highlight key themes, and even suggest connections between ideas, fostering creativity. Additionally, AI can generate summaries, track references, and maintain structured notes, ensuring no valuable insight is lost. With smart search functions and automated tagging, writers can quickly retrieve relevant data, streamlining the research process. Ultimately, AI enhances productivity, enabling authors to transform scattered information into well-organized, inspiring content.

3. Summary Notes:

If you prefer to keep things simple, writing summary notes is a great way to organise your research without being bogged down by too many details. This method involves writing concise summaries of your research material, highlighting only the most important information that is relevant to your writing.

For instance, if you're researching historical events for a novel, you might write a one-paragraph summary for each major event, detailing the key points. These summaries give you a quick reference guide when you're writing, allowing you to avoid having to re-read pages of notes. This method is also useful when you're reviewing a large number of sources, as it helps you focus on the information that is most important for your project.

The best method of organising research will depend on your personal preferences and the nature of your project. No matter which method you choose, the key is to stay organised and develop a system that works for you. This will not only save time but also make the process of writing more efficient and enjoyable.

References

Atwood, Margaret. *The Handmaid's Tale*. McClelland & Stewart, 1985.

Doerr, Anthony. *All the Light We Cannot See*. Scribner, 2014.

Eudora Welty. *The Eye of the Story : Selected Essays and Reviews*. Vintage International, 1990.

King, Stephen. *On Writing : A Memoir of the Craft*. Scribner, 2000, p. 145.

Lee, Harper. *To Kill a Mockingbird*. 1960. Chelsea House Publishers, 1960.

Mantel, Hilary. *Wolf Hall*. Editorial Presença, 2020.

Neil Degrasse Tyson. *Astrophysics for People in a Hurry*. W.W. Norton & Company, 2017.

Staff, Guardian. "Zadie Smith: 'I Have a Very Messy and Chaotic Mind.'" *The Guardian*, 21 Jan. 2018, www.theguardian.com/books/2018/jan/21/zadie-smith-you-ask-the-questions-self-doubt.

Chapter 3

Three Act Structure and Hero's Journey

Creative writing has a rich history. It has evolved over centuries into a powerful form of expression. It is the art of using words to tell stories, share emotions, and create imaginative worlds. Writers have tried to find different ways to tell stories that touch their readers on many levels. The purpose of creative writing has always remained the same; to connect with their readers and share meaningful experiences. Writers have experimented with different techniques to do the same and make their writings compelling. One of the most well-known techniques used in storytelling is Aristotle's *Three Act Structure* and Joseph Campbell's *Hero's Journey*. It is widely used in novels, plays, and films to shape the narrative into a compelling and coherent story. These models offer distinct yet complementary approaches to structuring narratives, each serving unique purposes in crafting memorable stories. This chapter will explain how these storytelling methods help in creating imaginative writings in modern age as well. Irrespective of the form of writing, these techniques of storytelling help create stories that will create a long-lasting impact on the readers.

3.1 What is the Three Act Structure?

The Three Act Structure, rooted in Aristotle's *Poetics*, represents one of the earliest and most foundational frameworks in storytelling. Aristotle's insights into dramatic structure have profoundly shaped narrative construction across various genres and mediums. According to Aristotle, a well-crafted story should have a clear beginning, middle, and end, each contributing to a cohesive narrative that elicits emotional engagement and catharsis from the audience.

Act One (The Beginning or the Setup)

The first act introduces the protagonist, establishes the setting, and presents the central conflict. It sets the stage for the narrative, providing the necessary background and context that allow readers to understand the characters' motivations and

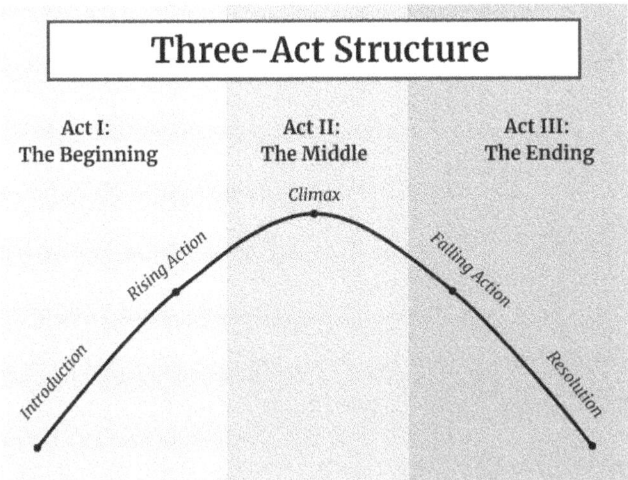

the stakes involved. This act is crucial for creating an emotional connection with the audience and establishing the groundwork for the subsequent development of the plot.

Key Elements of Act One:

Introduction of the Main Character(s): The protagonist (main character) is introduced, along with their personality, background, and goals. It's important that the audience understands who the main character is and what motivates them.

Setting the Scene: The writer establishes the time and place in which the story occurs. Whether it's a fantasy world, a historical setting, or a modern-day city, the audience needs to feel immersed in the environment.

The Inciting Incident: The inciting incident is the event that sets the story in motion. It is usually something that disrupts the normal life of the protagonist and pushes them into the main conflict of the story. For example, in a superhero story, the inciting incident might be when the hero discovers their powers or when a villain threatens the world.

The First Plot Point: Towards the end of Act One, there is a significant turning point that propels the protagonist into the main action of the story. This is often called the "First Plot Point" or "Turning Point One." It marks the transition from the setup to the confrontation in Act Two.

In F. Scott Fitzgerald's *The Great Gatsby*, Act One is where we are introduced to Nick Carraway, the novel's narrator, who recounts his experiences in the opulent world of West Egg. We encounter Jay Gatsby, the enigmatic millionaire with mysterious pasts, and Daisy Buchanan, the object of Gatsby's obsessive longing. This act establishes the primary setting and conflict, highlighting Gatsby's pursuit of the American Dream and his desire to rekindle his past romance with Daisy. The introduction of these elements sets the stage for the unfolding drama and prepares readers for the emotional journey that lies ahead.

Another example is, J.K. Rowling's *Harry Potter and the Philosopher's Stone*, in which Act One introduces us to Harry's ordinary life living with his aunt and uncle. The inciting incident is when Harry receives a letter inviting him to attend Hogwarts School of Witchcraft and Wizardry. The First Plot Point occurs when Harry chooses to leave his old life behind and enters the magical world.

Act Two (The Middle or the Confrontation)

Act Two is often the longest and the most complex part of the narrative. This act Showcases the protagonist's challenges and the escalation of tension. It is characterised by rising stakes, deeper character development, and a series of obstacles that test the protagonist's resolve. The central conflict intensifies as the protagonist faces increasing difficulties, leading to a greater investment in the narrative's outcome.

Key Elements of Act Two:

Rising Action: In Act Two, the story's tension increases as the protagonist faces more challenges. These challenges are not only external (physical obstacles, antagonists) but also internal (emotional struggles, self-doubt).

The Midpoint: Somewhere in the middle of Act Two, there is usually a key event called the Midpoint. This event changes the direction of the story, often forcing the protagonist to shift their strategy or face a new problem. The stakes are raised at this point, making the situation more urgent.

Character Development: Act Two is crucial for character development. The protagonist grows, learns new skills, and starts to change as a person. This is also the part of the story where relationships between characters develop and evolve.

The Second Plot Point: Towards the end of Act Two, there is another major turning point called the Second Plot Point or Turning Point Two. This event often brings the protagonist to their lowest point, where it seems like all is lost. However, it also sets the stage for the final act and the climax of the story.

Act Two of *The Great Gatsby* begins with Gatsby's reunion with Daisy, which sets off a chain of events that complicates his quest. The rekindled relationship with Daisy reveals the gap between Gatsby's idealized vision of the past and the reality of his present circumstances. Gatsby's attempts to recreate the past lead to conflicts with Tom Buchanan and other characters, deepening the story's emotional and narrative complexity. This act is marked by dramatic confrontations, misunderstandings, and escalating tension that culminate in a turning point or crisis moment.

Harry Potter and the Philosopher's Stone, after crossing into the magical world (First Plot Point), Harry begins his new life at Hogwarts, making friends (Ron, Hermione) and enemies (Draco, Snape). The midpoint occurs when Harry discovers the Philosopher's Stone is in danger and realises Voldemort is involved (raising the stakes). Harry, Ron, and Hermione work together to solve the mystery, facing obstacles like Fluffy, the enchanted chessboard, and the potions riddle.

Act Three (The Ending or the Resolution)

The final act brings the story to its climax and resolution. It is where the central conflict reaches its peak and is resolved, leading to the story's conclusion. This act provides closure and catharsis, allowing the audience to reflect on the journey and its implications.

Key Elements of Act Three:

The Climax: The climax is the most intense part of the story. It is the moment of greatest tension, where the protagonist faces their main challenge or antagonist. This is often a life-or-death moment, where the outcome of the story is decided.

The Resolution: After the climax, the story enters the resolution phase. This is where the loose ends are tied up, and we see how the protagonist's journey has affected them. They may return to their normal life or begin a new chapter with the lessons they have learned.

Character Transformation: Act Three often shows how the protagonist has changed as a result of their journey. Whether they have grown stronger, wiser, or more compassionate, the character transformation is a key aspect of a satisfying resolution.

The resolution in *The Great Gatsby* occurs as Gatsby's confrontation with Tom Buchanan exposes the futility of his dreams. The climax of Gatsby's struggle comes with the tragic unravelling of his aspirations and the eventual tragic end of his life. The resolution provides a moving reflection on the American Dream and the illusions that drive human behaviour. The story's conclusion elicits a profound sense of loss and reflection, embodying Aristotle's concept of catharsis by evoking a deep emotional response from the audience.

Similarly, in *Harry Potter and the Philosopher's Stone*, the climax happens when Harry confronts Quirrell (who is secretly hosting Voldemort) and prevents him from stealing the Stone. Harry's bravery, loyalty, and quick-thinking lead to Quirrell's defeat and Voldemort's temporary retreat. The falling action shows Dumbledore explaining events, Gryffindor winning the House Cup, and Harry returning to the Dursleys—but now with confidence in his identity as a wizard.

Aristotle's notion of catharsis—the emotional purging experienced by the audience—remains a key component of the Three Act Structure.

By following this structure, writers can craft narratives that not only engage readers but also leave a lasting impact, allowing them to process and reflect on the emotional journey of the characters.

The Three Act Structure works well because it mirrors the natural way we experience stories. We are introduced to a problem, watch as someone tries to solve it, and then see the outcome. This structure also keeps the audience engaged, as it builds tension and excitement in the middle, with a satisfying resolution at the end. The Three Act Structure is also flexible. While it provides a general framework, writers can play with it, adding subplots, shifting the emphasis of each act, or even blending genres. Understanding the Three Act Structure gives you a strong foundation for building a compelling narrative.

3.2 The Hero's Journey

While the Three Act Structure emphasizes external plot progression, The Hero's Journey, also known as the Monomyth, was popularized by American mythologist Joseph Campbell in his book *The Hero with a Thousand Faces*. Campbell observed that myths from different cultures across the world shared a similar structure, one that followed a single hero who embarks on an adventure, faces trials, and ultimately returns transformed. This universal pattern, the Hero's Journey, can be found in ancient myths, religious stories, and modern creative writing, including novels, films, and even video games.

In creative writing, the Hero's Journey serves as a roadmap for character development and plot progression. It revolves around the growth of a protagonist who faces challenges, overcomes obstacles, and experiences personal transformation. This structure is often used in fantasy, adventure, and science fiction genres but can also be adapted for other types of stories. It is more than a series of events; it's a profound exploration of the human experience. The hero often starts as an ordinary individual, but through the challenges they face and the trials they endure, they undergo significant internal transformation. Campbell's concept, drawn from his study of comparative mythology, outlines this journey in distinct stages, often referred to as the cycle of *departure, initiation*, and *return*. In essence, the hero leaves their familiar world, encounters trials that test their strength and resolve, and ultimately returns transformed, bearing newfound wisdom or power.

The beauty of the Hero's Journey lies in its adaptability. It is not confined to ancient myths or epic tales; it can be found in modern literature, film, and even video games. From classic tales like *The Odyssey* and *Beowulf*, to contemporary stories such as *The Lord of the Rings* or *Star Wars*, the structure of the Hero's Journey continues to resonate with audiences because it reflects a fundamental aspect of the human condition: the desire for growth, understanding, and transformation. Hero's Journey was further developed into 12 stages of the Hero's journey by screenwriter Christopher Vogler.

The Ordinary World

The Ordinary World represents the hero's initial state before the adventure begins. It is the hero's everyday life, characterized by familiarity and routine. This stage establishes the hero's normalcy and sets the stage for the forthcoming changes.

To understand it better, let's take an example of J.R.R. Tolkien's *The Hobbit*. In this book Bilbo Baggins starts in the peaceful and uneventful Shire. His life is marked by comfort and predictability, which contrasts sharply with the adventure that awaits him. This initial setting provides a stark juxtaposition to the extraordinary experiences Bilbo will encounter, highlighting the significance of his journey and transformation.

The Call to Adventure

The Call to Adventure introduces the hero to a challenge or quest that disrupts their Ordinary World. This stage sets the narrative in motion by presenting the hero with an opportunity for change and growth. Bilbo receives the Call to Adventure when Gandalf and the dwarves arrive at his doorstep, inviting him to join their quest to reclaim their homeland from the dragon Smaug. This call challenges Bilbo's comfortable life and propels him into a world of danger and discovery. The Call to Adventure is a pivotal moment that motivates the hero to step out of their comfort zone and embrace the unknown.

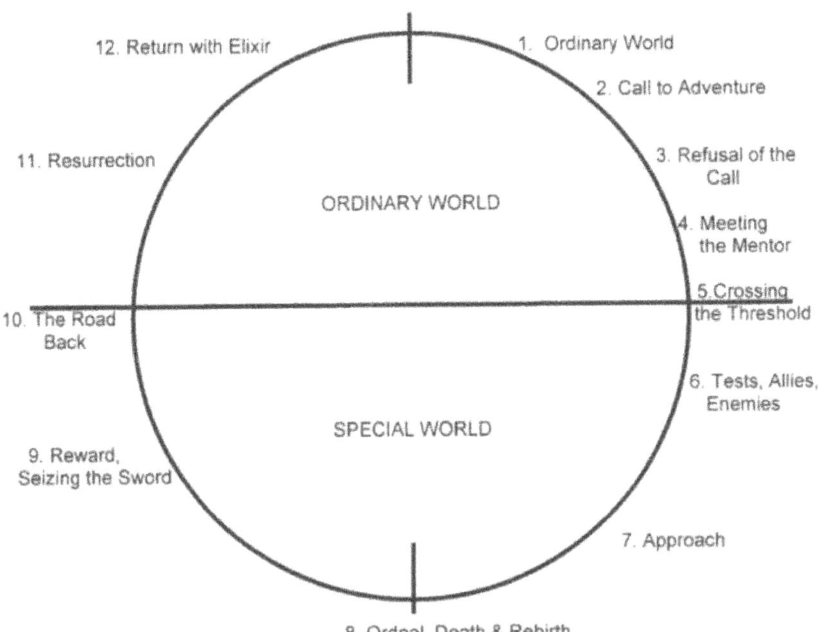

Refusal of the Call

Often, the hero initially resists the call to adventure due to fear, doubt, or reluctance. This stage highlights the hero's internal conflict and reluctance to leave their familiar world. Bilbo's initial response to the Call to Adventure is one of hesitation and reluctance. He is apprehensive about leaving the Shire and embarking on a dangerous quest. This reluctance emphasizes Bilbo's ordinary nature and the magnitude of the journey he is about to undertake. The refusal serves as a dramatic pause before the hero fully commits to the adventure.

Meeting the Mentor

The mentor figure provides guidance, support, and wisdom to the hero. This character helps the hero navigate the challenges of the journey and offers encouragement and resources. Gandalf serves as Bilbo's mentor in *The Hobbit*, providing him with valuable advice and support throughout the quest. Gandalf's role is crucial in preparing Bilbo for the challenges ahead, offering him the courage and tools necessary to succeed. The mentor's presence underscores the importance of guidance and support in the hero's journey.

Crossing the Threshold

Crossing the Threshold marks the hero's commitment to the adventure and departure from their Ordinary World. It signifies the beginning of the hero's transformation and immersion in the new world. Bilbo's Crossing the Threshold occurs when he leaves the Shire and joins the dwarves on their journey. This moment signifies Bilbo's commitment to the quest and his entry into a world of magic and danger. The crossing of the threshold is a symbolic transition from the familiar to the unknown, marking the beginning of Bilbo's transformative journey.

Tests, Allies, and Enemies

Throughout the journey, the hero encounters various tests, makes allies, and faces enemies. These challenges contribute to the hero's growth and development, shaping their character and abilities. Bilbo's journey is marked by encounters with numerous challenges and characters, including his encounter with Gollum, where he must use his wit to escape. He also makes allies, such as the dwarves and the elves, and faces enemies, including trolls and goblins. These experiences test his courage and resourcefulness, contributing to his growth as a character.

The Approach to the Inmost Cave

The Approach to the Inmost Cave represents the hero's preparation for a significant ordeal or confrontation. It is a stage of introspection and readiness for the ultimate challenge. Bilbo's approach to the Inmost Cave is his journey into the Lonely Mountain to confront the dragon Smaug. This stage involves facing the dangers and challenges leading up to the climactic confrontation. The approach symbolizes his readiness to face his greatest challenge and confront the central conflict of the story.

The Ordeal

The Ordeal is the hero's greatest challenge, often involving a symbolic or literal death and rebirth. It represents a critical turning point in the hero's journey and signifies the climax of their transformation.

Bilbo's ordeal is his confrontation with Smaug, where he must use his courage and resourcefulness to outwit the dragon and retrieve the treasure. This confrontation is a test of Bilbo's character and abilities, marking a significant moment in his transformation and growth.

The Reward

After overcoming the ordeal, the hero receives a reward or recognition. This reward signifies the hero's success and the benefits gained from their journey. Bilbo's reward is not only the treasure but also the confidence and self-worth he gains through his experiences. The reward represents the culmination of Bilbo's growth and the fruits of his efforts. It symbolizes the positive changes resulting from his journey.

The Road Back

The Road Back represents the hero's return journey to their Ordinary World, often involving additional challenges or obstacles. It signifies the transition from the adventure back to the familiar world. Bilbo's Road Back involves his return to the Shire after the quest, including the Battle of the Five Armies and the subsequent challenges.

The Resurrection

The Resurrection is the hero's final test or transformation, often involving a profound change or realization. It represents the culmination of the hero's journey and their new understanding or perspective. Bilbo's resurrection occurs when he returns to the Shire, having transformed from a timid hobbit into a wise and confident individual. This final stage symbolizes Bilbo's complete transformation and the lasting impact of his adventure on his character.

Return with the Elixir

The Return with the Elixir represents the hero's return home with newfound wisdom or treasure. It signifies the integration of the hero's journey into their Ordinary World and the benefits gained from their experiences. Bilbo returns to the Shire with not only the treasure but also the wisdom and confidence gained from his journey. The Elixir symbolizes the positive changes and growth that the hero brings back to their Ordinary World.

Writing Activity

The Hero's Journey Vocabulary Adventure

Ordinary World: Begin by describing your protagonist's everyday life before the adventure begins. Use descriptive adjectives to bring this world to life.

Call to Adventure: Write the scene where your hero receives the call, but this time focus on verbs. Use powerful, action-packed verbs to describe how this moment plays out. Do they hesitate, embrace, or dread this call?

Refusal of the Call: In this step, write a short internal monologue for your character where they express their fears or uncertainties. Make use of adverbs to describe how your character thinks or speaks.

Meeting the Mentor: Describe a conversation between the hero and their mentor using dialogue. Include words that capture the mentor's wisdom, perhaps using nouns that suggest knowledge, such as wisdom, insight, or guidance.

Crossing the Threshold: In a paragraph, focus on using prepositions to describe the movement through space. For example: "They stepped across the bridge, into the dark forest, and beyond the safety of home."

Tests, Allies, and Enemies: Write a scene where your hero encounters a challenge, and use conjunctions to build suspense and complexity in your sentence structure. For example: "They fought fiercely, but the enemy was relentless, and they soon realised they needed help."

The Ordeal and Reward: Write the climactic scene where your hero faces their biggest trial. Use strong, vivid vocabulary to describe them.

The Road Back & Resurrection: In this step, focus on your use of pronouns to tell the story smoothly. Describe how he/she/they overcomes this last hurdle and what they learn from it.

Return with the Elixir: Write the scene where your hero comes home, using nouns and adjectives to describe the change in both the character and their world.

Bonus Vocabulary Activity

After completing each step of your Hero's Journey, review your writing and highlight 10 new or unfamiliar words you used. For each word, write a definition, part of speech, and a sentence using that word in a new context.

3.3 Comparing Hero's Journey and Three Act Structure

While the Three Act Structure and the Hero's Journey both guide narrative construction, they serve distinct purposes and offer different perspectives on storytelling. The Three Act Structure primarily focuses on the external arc of the story, emphasizing pacing, plot progression, and the resolution of conflict. On the other hand, the Hero's Journey emphasis on the protagonist's internal transformation and personal growth, mapping a more introspective and symbolic path. While both frameworks can overlap, with the Three Act Structure providing clear stages for plot development and the Hero's Journey enriching character evolution, each offers a unique approach to shaping narrative. Together, they allow writers to balance the emotional depth of the characters with the structural clarity of the plot.

Focus on Plot vs. Character

The Three Act Structure primarily focuses on the external progression of events, providing a framework for organizing the narrative's plot. It emphasizes the sequence of events and the resolution of conflicts, offering a clear and structured approach to storytelling.

The Hero's Journey, on the other hand, emphasizes the protagonist's internal transformation and growth. It explores the hero's psychological and emotional journey, highlighting their evolution and self-discovery. This focus on character development offers a deeper exploration of the hero's personal change and the impact of the journey on their identity.

Flexibility and Depth

The Three Act Structure is often more straightforward and adaptable, making it suitable for various genres and storytelling styles. Its simplicity and flexibility allow writers to organise their narratives effectively, regardless of genre or complexity. The Hero's Journey, with its intricate stages and mythological roots, offers a more in-depth exploration of character transformation. It is particularly effective for stories with significant internal change and development, providing a rich framework for character-driven narratives.

Character Transformation vs. External Conflict

The Hero's Journey places a strong emphasis on character transformation, exploring how the protagonist changes through their experiences. It delves into the psychological and emotional impact of the journey, highlighting the hero's growth and self-discovery. The Three Act Structure, while also addressing character development, focuses more on external events and conflicts. It emphasizes the progression of the plot and the resolution of conflicts, providing a framework for organizing the narrative's structure.

Both the Three-Act Structure and the Hero's Journey offer valuable frameworks for constructing compelling narratives in creative writing. Each structure provides writers with a clear path to follow, ensuring that stories maintain a sense of direction, purpose, and emotional resonance. While these two structures serve distinct purposes, they are not mutually exclusive. Writers can adapt and blend elements from both, depending on the story they want to tell and the emotional impact they seek to create.

References

Campbell, Joseph. *The Hero with a Thousand Faces*. New World Library, 2008.

Fitzgerald, F. Scott. *The Great Gatsby*. Scribner, 2004.

Rowling, J.K. *Harry Potter and the Philosopher's Stone*. Bloomsbury, 1997.

Tolkien, J.R.R. *The Hobbit, or There and Back Again*. Houghton Mifflin Harcourt, 2001.

Vogler, Christopher. *The Writer's Journey: Mythic Structure for Writers*. 3rd ed., Michael Wiese Productions, 2007.

Chapter 4

Character Development in Creative Writing

In creative writing, without characters, story, theme, dialogue, or setting will make no sense. They complete the world of stories. They give life to the narrative, drive the plot, and connect the audience to the fictional world. For readers to relate to the story, they will need characters they can relate to. Character development refers to the process of creating a character with depth, complexity, and evolution, so they feel real to the readers. A well-developed character is more than just a name and a few descriptive traits—they have desires, motivations, flaws, and personalities that grow throughout the story. Character development is employed during the active process of the writing. This chapter will look into the details on where characters come from, how to develop them, the essential elements that make them compelling, and the role of conflict and motivation in shaping them.

> "A writer should create living people: people, not characters. A character is a caricature."
>
> _Ernest Hemingway

4.1 Where Do Characters Come From?

Characters can come to a writer in different ways. Some are carefully crafted to serve a thematic purpose, while others may appear spontaneously, often emerging from the writer's subconscious mind. Regardless of the method of creation, characters need to serve the narrative and offer a personal connection to the themes and emotions of the story.

Thematic Characters

Some characters are born out of the themes or ideas that the writer wants to explore. These characters act as vessels for larger social, cultural, or philosophical issues. For instance, in George Orwell's dystopian masterpiece, *1984*, Winston Smith is not merely a character but a representation of resistance against an oppressive regime. His struggle for individuality within a totalitarian state mirrors the broader themes of surveillance, control, and the loss of personal freedoms. Writers may use such characters to comment on issues that affect society, such as freedom, justice, or morality.

Similarly, in Charles Dickens' *A Tale of Two Cities*, Sydney Carton embodies the theme of personal redemption. His ultimate sacrifice for the sake of another character, Lucie Manette, illustrates the transformative power of selflessness and the possibility of personal redemption through heroic acts.

Creating thematic characters gives the writer a clear direction from the start. When a character represents a larger issue, it becomes easier to flesh out their traits and motivations because the writer knows why the character exists and what point they are trying to make. However, it's important to balance this approach so that the character remains relatable and doesn't become just a symbol without human complexity. While Winston Smith in *1984* represents resistance, his personal struggles and emotional depth make him a fully realised character rather than a mere vehicle for thematic exploration.

Spontaneous Characters

In contrast to thematic characters, spontaneous characters emerge spontaneously from the writer's mind. These characters may not have been planned or intellectually crafted, but they appear due to a sudden inspiration or a deep need from the writer's unconscious. According to psychoanalysis, the unconscious mind constantly processes thoughts and emotions that may later burst into conscious awareness. Writers who tap into this can create characters that feel deeply personal and human because they are shaped by the writer's own experiences, emotions, and psyche.

Spontaneous characters can be a powerful resource for writers, as they often provide insight into the writer's inner world. Writing these characters may help the writer discover new things about themselves and add layers of depth to the narrative. Because these characters are born out of emotion and intuition, they often feel more authentic.

4.2 Developing a Character

Once a character is conceived, the process of development begins. This means adding layers to their personality, understanding their motivations, and giving them realistic traits and backgrounds. To successfully develop a character, writers need to ask essential questions about their character's identity, their role in the story, and how they interact with the world around them.

Essential Questions for Character Development

What is the character's age?

Age plays a critical role in determining how a character sees the world and the experiences they've had. For instance, in Jane Austen's *Pride and Prejudice*, Elizabeth Bennet's youthful idealism and observations of societal norms are shaped by her age, influencing her interactions and development throughout the novel. A child will have a different perspective from an adult, and an elderly person may have a broader view of life than a teenager. As in J.K. Rowling's *Harry Potter* series, Harry Potter's maturation from a young, insecure boy into a confident young adult is pivotal to the story's progression. Knowing the age of a character helps the writer decide what knowledge, freedoms, and limitations the character has.

What is the character's gender?

Gender influences the way a character experiences the world and how they are socialized. It can also determine the societal expectations placed on them. Take for example, Virginia Woolf's *Orlando*, the protagonist's gender transformation challenges traditional gender norms and reflects on the fluidity of identity. Understanding how a character's gender impacts their life is crucial for crafting authentic portrayals. Gender can affect a character's opportunities, relationships, and societal roles, shaping their experiences and behaviours throughout the narrative.

What is their family background?

Family background shapes a person's early experiences, their sense of belonging, and how they relate to others. Was the character raised in a supportive environment, or did they grow up in a dysfunctional household? Do they have a close-knit family, or are they independent? These factors influence the character's emotional landscape and relationships with others. For example, in William Faulkner's *The Sound and the Fury*, the Compson family's dysfunctional dynamics deeply affect each character's psyche and behaviour. Similarly, in Harper Lee's *To Kill a Mockingbird*, Scout Finch's relationship with her father, Atticus, and their family's values significantly influence her moral development.

Writing Prompt: Rewriting a Classic Character for 21st century

Reimagine the character of Mr. Darcy from Pride and Prejudice as a modern-day figure living in the 21st century.

Task: Character Profile Update:

Age: How old is modern-day Mr. Darcy, and how does his age influence his lifestyle, ambitions, and perspective on relationships in today's world?

Profession: What is Mr. Darcy's profession or field of work in the 21st century? Is he a tech entrepreneur, a lawyer, or perhaps a successful architect? Consider how his career reflects his status and personality.

Social Status: Mr. Darcy was a wealthy landowner in the original novel. How would his wealth and social standing translate into modern times? Does he come from old money, or has he built his wealth himself?

Personality: *Mr. Darcy's reserved and aloof nature is central to his character. How does this play out in a world of social media, instant communication, and modern dating? Is he still quiet and distant, or does he have a different way of expressing his feelings?*

Romantic Relationships: *In the 21st century, what are Mr. Darcy's views on relationships, love, and marriage? Does he believe in traditional values, or has his perspective evolved with the times? How would his relationship with a modern-day Elizabeth Bennet unfold?*

What are the character's key life experiences?

Life experiences are vital for understanding a character's motivations and behaviour. Significant events—such as losses, achievements, traumas, or moments of joy—shape how a character views the world and what drives them forward. Take the character of Jay Gatsby from *The Great Gatsby* as an example. His rags-to-riches journey and his longing for Daisy Buchanan are rooted in his past experiences and aspirations. These experiences drive his actions and illuminate his motivations, making him a more complex and relatable character.

Where does the character fit in within the moral scheme of the story?

This question is important because every character, whether they're a hero, a villain, or something in between, operates within a specific moral framework. What is their personal code of ethics? What do they believe is right or wrong, and how does this shape their decisions throughout the story? These questions are crucial for developing a coherent and relatable character arc. The character of Dorothea Brooke in George Eliot's *Middlemarch,* goes through moral and ethical dilemmas, including her struggle with societal expectations and personal fulfillment. This plays a crucial role in her character arc and the story's thematic exploration. A character's moral framework influences their decisions, actions, and interactions with others, contributing to their overall development and the narrative's progression.

Write a Scene:

Set Mr. Darcy in a contemporary setting (e.g., a bustling corporate office, an exclusive party in a city penthouse, or a quiet coffee shop). Show how his character traits (pride, reserve, sense of duty) would manifest in today's world. Focus on dialogue and inner thoughts to reveal his internal conflict, especially in his interactions with a modern-day Elizabeth. How does his pride or social awkwardness affect his relationships with others in a fast-paced, digital age? Write 300-500 words where Mr. Darcy is faced with a situation that forces him to confront his feelings for Elizabeth (or a modern equivalent). Use this scene to reflect how his classic characteristics adapt to current-day challenges.

4.3 Character Motivation

One of the most crucial aspects of character development is understanding a character's motivation—the driving force behind their actions and decisions. Motivation provides the foundation for why characters do what they do, shaping their behaviours, relationships, and responses to the events around them. Without a clear motivation, characters can come across as flat, aimless, or unconvincing, as their actions will lack purpose. To create well-rounded, believable characters, it's essential to identify what they want to achieve and why they want it.

Motivation can stem from a variety of sources. It could be a desire for personal success, love, revenge, power, or freedom, or even the need to protect loved ones or correct a past mistake. Understanding these deeper desires gives writers insight into how a character might react in different situations. It also makes characters relatable; readers connect with characters whose motivations reflect real human emotions and struggles.

Moreover, motivations can evolve over time, adding complexity and growth to a character's arc. For instance, a character may start with a selfish goal but, through experience, shift toward a more selfless one. This evolution keeps readers engaged, as they witness the character's transformation and the consequences of their desires.

Conflicting motivations between characters also generate tension, driving the plot forward. When motivations collide, whether internally or externally, it leads to conflict, which is a key element in any story. Therefore, understanding motivation not only enhances character development but also strengthens the overall narrative by providing direction, conflict, and emotional depth that keeps the audience invested in the characters' journeys.

Motivation can be of two types: Outer Motivation and Inner Motivation.

Outer Motivation

Outer motivation refers to the external goal that the character is working toward. This is something tangible and concrete, such as winning a competition, finding a lost treasure, or defeating an antagonist. Outer motivation often drives the plot because the character's actions and choices are centered around achieving this goal.

In *The Lord of the Rings*, Frodo's outer motivation is to destroy the One Ring and save Middle-earth. This goal gives him a clear path to follow, and the audience is able to understand his journey. Similarly, in Herman Melville's *Moby-Dick*, Captain Ahab's outer motivation is his quest for vengeance against the white whale, Moby Dick. This pursuit propels the narrative and shapes Ahab's interactions with the crew and the sea. Outer motivations often drive the plot and create a sense of urgency and direction in the narrative. In Suzanne Collins' *The Hunger Games*, Katniss Everdeen's goal to survive the arena and protect her sister drives the plot and her actions. Outer motivations provide a clear sense of purpose for characters and guide their actions throughout the story.

Inner Motivation

Inner motivation, on the other hand, is the deeper, emotional reason behind why the character wants to achieve their goal. This is not just about what the character wants but why they want it. Inner motivation is often linked to the character's personal struggles, insecurities, or desires for self-improvement. In Emily Brontë's *Wuthering Heights*, Heathcliff's desire for revenge against those who wronged him is intertwined with his own feelings of rejection and loss. This emotional complexity adds depth to his character and motives. Inner motivations often reveal the character's internal struggles, fears, and desires, adding layers to their personality and enriching the narrative. In *The Bell Jar* by Sylvia Plath, Esther Greenwood's inner motivation is influenced by her struggle with mental illness and the search for personal identity. Her internal conflicts and desires reflect her emotional turmoil and provide insight into her character's development.

For writers, getting these two levels of motivation to work in harmony is crucial. It enriches character development, making characters feel more lifelike and multidimensional. A character's external goal may be fuelled by a deeper emotional need, and as they pursue their outer motivation, their inner journey becomes equally significant. By balancing both outer and inner motivations, writers can create characters who are not only active in driving the plot but also emotionally resonant with readers. The fusion of outer and inner motivations helps to shape well-rounded, believable characters that leave a lasting impact on the audience.

Writing Prompt

Rewrite Macbeth's motivations from Shakespeare's Macbeth. Instead of his ambition to become king driving his actions, imagine that Macbeth's outer motivation is to protect Scotland from an impending external invasion. His inner motivation could stem from a deep sense of loyalty to his country or a desire to right past wrongs in his family history. Reimagine how this altered motivation would impact his decisions, relationships with other characters, and his tragic downfall.

4.4 The Role of Conflict in Character Development

Conflict is a crucial element in character development because it challenges your character and helps them evolve. Without conflict, characters would have no reason to change or grow, and the story would lack tension and interest. It pushes characters out of their comfort zones, forcing them to make decisions, face their fears, or confront challenges. It adds tension and excitement to a story. These struggles are what help shape the character's journey, giving them the opportunity to evolve. When a character faces obstacles, whether it's dealing with personal fears, difficult relationships, or challenging circumstances, they are forced to make decisions. These decisions reveal who they are, what they value, and how they change over time. Without conflict, a character might remain static, but with it, they are given the chance to develop, becoming more complex and relatable. For example, a character dealing with a tough decision about loyalty or ambition must weigh their options and take action, showing their growth throughout the story.

Conflict also serves to keep readers engaged. It introduces uncertainty and unpredictability, making the reader wonder what will happen next and how the character will handle the pressure. The character's responses to these challenges help build their personality, revealing their strengths, weaknesses, and resilience. Conflict is not just about creating problems for the character but about offering opportunities for them to grow and change. Whether they succeed or fail, the way they handle difficult situations defines their journey and leaves a lasting impact on who they are by the end of the story.

Conflict can be divided into two main types: Outer Conflict and Inner Conflict.

Outer Conflict

Outer conflict refers to the external obstacles or challenges that the character must face. These are events, situations, or antagonists that stand in the way of the character's goal. Outer conflict is often action-driven and includes struggles such as battles, difficult situations, or conflicts with other characters. In *The Hunger Games*, Katniss Everdeen faces numerous external conflicts, from surviving the deadly arena to battling against a corrupt government. These outer conflicts influence the character's development. As Katniss faces life-threatening situations, she grows stronger, braver, and more determined.

In William Golding's *The Lord of the Flies*, the boys' struggle to maintain order and civilization on the island creates intense external conflicts that drive the plot and reveal the darker aspects of their nature. The external conflicts faced by the boys highlight their inherent flaws and fears, ultimately leading to a breakdown of their societal constructs and the emergence of their primal instincts.

Inner Conflict

While outer conflict deals with external challenges, inner conflict focuses on the character's internal struggles. Inner conflict is about the character's doubts, fears, insecurities, and moral dilemmas. It often revolves around difficult decisions or the emotional and psychological turmoil that the character experiences as they navigate the story's challenges. Take *Hamlet* as an example. The protagonist's inner conflict revolves around his hesitation to take revenge on his uncle for murdering his father. Hamlet is torn between his moral duty to seek justice and his fear of the consequences of committing murder. This internal struggle adds complexity to Hamlet's character and drives the narrative's exploration of themes such as revenge, morality, and existentialism. In Fyodor Dostoevsky's *Crime and Punishment*, Raskolnikov's internal conflict over his crime and its moral implications drives much of the novel's tension. His feelings of guilt and the search for redemption reveal his psychological turmoil and provide a deeper understanding of his character.

Inner conflict often adds emotional complexity and relatability to characters, making their journeys more compelling and their struggles more profound. Inner conflict adds emotional depth to a character. It allows the audience to see the character's vulnerability, making them more relatable and human. A character facing inner conflict is often more compelling because they are not just dealing with external forces but also wrestling with their own emotions and decisions.

Balancing Outer and Inner Conflict

The best character development often comes from a balance between outer and inner conflict. When both types of conflict are present, the character's journey becomes more dynamic and engaging. Outer conflict pushes the character to take action, while inner conflict forces them to reflect on their decisions and question their motivations.

An example is of the character Jane from Charlotte Brontë's *Jane Eyre*, where her external conflicts include her struggles with societal norms, personal hardships, and her tumultuous relationship with Mr. Rochester. Simultaneously, her inner conflicts involve her quest for self-respect, moral integrity, and emotional fulfillment. This combination of external and internal conflicts deepens Jane's character and contributes to the novel's exploration of themes such as love, independence, and social justice.

The way a character deals with both external and internal conflicts shape their growth. Conflict forces the character to adapt, learn, or change in some way, making their journey more engaging for the reader. Whether they succeed or fail in overcoming these conflicts, the experience leaves a lasting impact on who they are by the end of the story. In this way, conflict is not just about creating drama; it's about driving character development and shaping the overall narrative.

Writing Prompt: Exploring Conflict in Character Development

Select a character from any literary work of your choice (e.g., Elizabeth Bennet from Pride and Prejudice, or Jay Gatsby from The Great Gatsby).

1. ***Identify the Outer Conflicts:*** *Outline at least two significant external challenges or obstacles the character faces in the story. Describe how these conflicts impact their actions and relationships with other characters.*

2. ***Explore the Inner Conflicts:*** *Analyse at least two internal struggles or dilemmas the character experiences. How do*

these inner conflicts influence their decisions and personal growth?

3. ***Balance the Conflicts:*** *Write a short scene (300-500 words) where you illustrate how the character's outer and inner conflicts interact. Show how the resolution of one type of conflict affects the other. For example, if your character resolves an external conflict, how does it impact their internal struggles or vice versa?*

4. ***Reflect on Development:*** *Conclude with a brief reflection (150-200 words) on how balancing outer and inner conflicts contributes to the character's overall development and depth.*

4.5 Character Arc: The Transformation

A key element of character development is the character arc, which is the transformation a character goes through during the story. This arc shows how the character changes or grows, often learning important lessons about themselves and the world around them. A well-written character arc allows the character to evolve in meaningful ways, whether it's by gaining a new perspective, adjusting their behaviour, or shifting their motivations. At the start of the story, a character may have certain beliefs, attitudes, or desires, but as they face different challenges and experiences, these aspects of their personality may begin to change. For example, a character who starts off selfish or afraid might learn the value of compassion or courage by the end of the story. This journey of change helps make the character feel more real and relatable to readers. It adds depth to their personality and makes their journey more engaging. A well-developed character arc also enhances the overall story, as it connects the character's personal growth with the plot, creating a more satisfying and complete narrative. In the end, the character arc is what gives the story emotional weight and makes the character's journey memorable.

Types of Character Arcs

Positive Arc: In a positive character arc, the character begins the story with flaws, doubts, or a lack of confidence. Over the course of the story, they grow and change for the better, becoming stronger and more capable. Often, they face challenges that help them overcome their internal struggles, such as fear, insecurity, or self-doubt. By the end of the story, they have learned valuable lessons and become a better person. Take for example, *Harry Potter series*. In the book series, Harry starts out as a lonely boy who doesn't know much about his place in the world. He feels unsure of himself and struggles with his identity. But as the story progresses, he faces difficult situations, makes strong friendships, and learns to embrace who he is. Through these experiences, Harry becomes a confident leader who accepts his role in the fight against Voldemort, the story's main villain.

A positive character arc shows personal growth and improvement, making the character more likable and relatable. It also creates a sense of satisfaction for the reader, as they witness the character overcome their struggles and reach their full potential. In the end, a positive arc leaves the character in a much better place than where they started.

Negative Arc: In a negative character arc, the character's journey takes a darker turn. Instead of growing stronger or better, they begin to lose hope, give in to their weaknesses, or become corrupted by their flaws. Over the course of the story, they move further away from who they once were, often making choices that lead them down a tragic path. This kind of arc focuses on the negative aspects of human nature, showing how someone can change for the worse.

A well-known example of a negative arc is Anakin Skywalker in *Star Wars*. He starts out as a brave and noble Jedi, committed to fighting for good. However, over time, he struggles with fear, anger, and a desire for power. These feelings drive him to make destructive choices, eventually leading him to become the villainous Darth Vader. His transformation is heartbreaking because, despite his potential to be a hero, he succumbs to the darker side of his character.

Negative arcs highlight the consequences of giving in to personal flaws or external pressures. While they often lead to a tragic or unhappy ending, they also explore the complexity of human emotions and decisions, making them powerful and thought-provoking stories.

Flat Arc: In a flat character arc, the character stays mostly the same throughout the story. Unlike other characters who might change or grow, a flat-arc character is confident in their beliefs and values from the start. They don't go through a personal transformation, but their presence and actions have a big effect on the world and people around them. A classic example of this is *Indiana Jones*. In his adventures, Indiana doesn't change much as a person—he starts and ends the story with the same personality and beliefs. However, the things he does and the choices he makes have a huge impact on the story's events and the other characters involved. His actions lead to big changes in the world around him, even though he himself remains steady.

Flat-arc characters are important because they often inspire or help other characters to change, or they may stand up against challenges without needing to change themselves. Their stability and strength in their beliefs drive the story forward and leave a lasting impact on the world they inhabit.

4.6 Creating Realistic and Relatable Characters

While the plot is what moves the story forward, it's the characters that make the audience truly care about what happens. A good story needs more than just events or action—it needs characters that feel real and relatable. When the audience can connect with the characters, they become invested in their journey, challenges, and outcomes. To do this, the writer must create characters that seem like real people, with strengths, flaws, emotions, and desires. These characters should have their own unique personalities, goals, and problems. When a character feels human, the audience can relate to them and understand their struggles and achievements, even if they live in a completely different world or situation. For example, a character who faces challenges, makes mistakes, or grows over time feels more relatable because we all experience these things in life. By developing

> "Remember that you don't write a story because you have an idea but because you have a believable character."
>
> _Flannery O'Connor

characters that feel genuine, writers allow readers to emotionally engage with the story, making it more powerful and memorable. To create realistic and relatable characters, writers need to focus on several aspects.

Flaws and Weaknesses: Perfect characters are often unrelatable. Giving a character flaws—whether it's insecurity, selfishness, or stubbornness—makes them more human and allows for character growth. For example, in Charles Dickens' *Great Expectations*, Pip's flaws, including his vanity and ambition, make him a more relatable and human character. His imperfections drive his development and make his journey of personal growth more compelling. Flaws also serve to humanize characters and make their struggles more relatable, like the character Emma from Jane Austen's *Emma*. The protagonist's misguided matchmaking and self-centred behaviour reflect her flaws and contribute to her growth throughout the novel. These imperfections create opportunities for character development and make the character's journey more engaging and authentic.

Emotions: Characters should feel real emotions and respond to situations in believable ways. Whether it's fear, joy, anger, or sadness, emotional depth connects the character to the audience. In *The Color Purple* by Alice Walker, Celie's emotional journey from oppression to self-discovery connects deeply with readers. Her experiences of trauma, resilience, and personal growth evoke empathy and allow readers to relate to her struggles and triumphs. Emotional depth adds complexity to characters and enhances their relatability. Characters who display authentic emotions and vulnerabilities become more relatable and engaging.

Consistency: A character should remain consistent with their established traits and motivations. While growth and change are important, characters should not behave in ways that contradict their core beliefs unless there's a strong reason. In *The Alchemist* by Paulo Coelho, Santiago consistently embodies curiosity and a desire to follow his dreams. From the beginning, his decision to seek out his Personal Legend drives the narrative. Throughout his journey, Santiago's commitment to listening to his heart and pursuing his vision of treasure reflects his core values. This consistency in his character, despite the challenges he faces, makes his growth and eventual realizations about life and destiny resonate deeply with readers.

Relationships: Characters are often defined by their relationships with others. The way they interact with family, friends, enemies, and love interests shapes their behaviour and reveals their true selves. Take an example of the relationships between the March sisters in Louisa May Alcott's *Little Women*. It shapes their development and reveal their individual personalities. The dynamics of their interactions provide insight into their values, ambitions, and growth.

Mariam from *A Thousand Splendid Suns* by Khaled Hosseini is another good example. Her relationships with her mother, Nana, and later with Laila significantly shape her character development. Her bond with Nana reveals Mariam's feelings of abandonment and her struggle for acceptance, which influences her self-worth throughout her life. In contrast, her relationship with Laila evolves into a deep friendship that transforms Mariam's understanding of love and sacrifice. This connection highlights Mariam's strength and resilience as she learns to prioritize Laila's well-being over her own fears. These relationships enrich Mariam's character, illustrating her growth from a girl seeking validation to a woman who finds strength in compassion and loyalty.

In creative writing, strong character development is essential for creating stories that truly resonate with readers. Characters need to feel real and relatable, and this requires careful thought about their backgrounds, motivations, and growth throughout the story. Whether characters are inspired by themes or arise spontaneously, they should be crafted with attention to detail. Writers should ask important questions about their characters' lives, such as what drives them and what challenges they face. Understanding these motivations helps to shape their journeys and makes their actions more believable.

Mastering character development is what transforms a good story into a great one. Well-crafted characters who undergo meaningful journeys can leave a lasting impression on readers. By exploring the origins of their characters, giving them realistic traits, and understanding the impact of their relationships, writers can create dynamic and memorable figures. These characters will resonate with readers long after the story ends, making the effort put into their development truly worthwhile.

References

Alcott, Louisa May. *Little Women*. Penguin Classics, 2009.

Austen, Jane. *Emma*. Penguin Classics, 2003.

Austen, Jane. *Pride and Prejudice*. Penguin Classics, 2002.

Bronte, Charlotte. *Jane Eyre*. Penguin Classics, 2006.

Bronte, Emily. *Wuthering Heights*. Oxford University Press, 2008.

Coelho, Paulo. *The Alchemist*. HarperOne, 1993.

Collins, Suzanne. *The Hunger Games*. Scholastic Press, 2008.

Dickens, Charles. *A Tale of Two Cities*. Penguin Classics, 2003.

Dickens, Charles. *Great Expectations*. Penguin Classics, 2003.

Eliot, George. *Middlemarch*. Penguin Classics, 2003.

Fitzgerald, F. Scott. *The Great Gatsby*. Scribner, 2004.

Golding, William. *Lord of the Flies*. Penguin Books, 2003.

Hosseini, Khaled. *A Thousand Splendid Suns*. Riverhead Books, 2007.

Melville, Herman. *Moby-Dick; or, The Whale*. Penguin Classics, 2002.

Orwell, George. *1984*. Signet Classics, 1961.

Plath, Sylvia. *The Bell Jar*. Harper Perennial Modern Classics, 2005.

Tolkien, J.R.R. *The Lord of the Rings*. Houghton Mifflin Harcourt, 2005.

Walker, Alice. *The Color Purple*. Mariner Books, 2003.

Woolf, Virginia. *Orlando: A Biography*. Mariner Books, 2006.

62

Part II:

Crafting Different Forms of Writing

Chapter 5

Writing Poetry

Poetry is not just writing rhyming words. It is a space where language is shaped into something more than just words on a page. It is where every line, every word carries weight, and nothing is wasted. Poetry is about exploring deeper human emotions and feelings and expressing it in a way that resonates deeply. The beauty of poetry lies in its simplicity and complexity all at once — a handful of words can evoke a universe of meaning. Poetry refines life into something that can be felt as much as it can be read.

> **Poetry is when an emotion has found its thought and the thought has found words.**
>
> **_Robert Frost**

The power of poetry comes from its ability to take ordinary language and transform it into something extraordinary. Poets have the gift of seeing the world differently, of finding beauty in places where others might see only the mundane. In poetry, words are chosen carefully, rhythm is crafted intentionally, and images are used to evoke emotion. As T.S. Eliot put it, *"Genuine poetry can communicate before it is understood."* (Eliot 206 It speaks to something deep within us that doesn't always need explanation.

There are many forms that poetry can take, each with its own rules and possibilities. From the traditional sonnet to free verse, from haiku to spoken word, poetry offers endless ways to express yourself. In each form, the poet finds a balance between structure and freedom. As Emily Dickinson once wrote, *"If I read a book and it makes my whole body so cold no fire can ever warm me, I know that is poetry. If I feel physically as if the top of my head were taken off, I know that is poetry. These are the only ways I know it. Is there any other way?"* (Dickinson 473)

5.1. The Power of Language in Poetry

Techniques like metaphor, simile, alliteration, and imagery are tools that poets use to make their words come alive. W.H. Auden noted, *"A poet is, before anything else, a person who is passionately in love with language."* (Auden 27) This love of language shines through in every carefully crafted line, transforming the ordinary into something profound.

Language in poetry is not merely a vessel for conveying meaning but an instrument for evoking profound emotional and sensory experiences. The choice of words, their arrangement, and their rhythm can transform a simple idea into a powerful statement.

American poet Robert Frost said, *"Poetry is when an emotion has found its thought and the thought has found words."* (Frost 776) This quote encapsulates the idea that poetry marries emotion with language, crafting a bridge between the internal and external worlds. Frost's own work, such as *"The Road Not Taken,"* demonstrates how language can embody complex human experiences and choices with simplicity and elegance. Consider the opening lines:

> *Two roads diverged in a yellow wood,*
> *And sorry I could not travel both*
> *And be one traveller, long I stood*
> *And looked down one as far as I could*
> *To where it bent in the undergrowth;*

Here, Frost uses straightforward language and imagery to explore the theme of choice and its consequences. The simplicity of the language allows readers to project their own experiences onto the poem, making it universally relatable.

William Wordsworth proclaimed, *"Poetry is the spontaneous overflow of powerful feelings: it takes its origin from emotion recollected in tranquillity"* (Preface to Lyrical Ballads, xxi-xxii). This overflow of emotion is meticulously channelled through the precision of language, making every word and phrase a deliberate choice. He also exemplifies the power of language in evoking nature's sublime beauty and personal reflection. Wordsworth's use of vivid imagery and contemplative language invites readers to share in his profound emotional experience. Wordsworth's work, such as in "*Lines Composed a Few Miles Above Tintern Abbey*," showcases his ability to evoke nature's sublime beauty and personal reflection:

> *Five years have passed; five summers, with the length*
> *Of five long winters! and again I hear*
> *These waters, rolling from their mountain-springs*
> *With a sweet inland murmur.—Once again*
> *Do I behold these steep and lofty cliffs,*
> *Which on a wild secluded scene impress*
> *Thoughts of more deep seclusion; and connect*
> *The landscape with the quiet of the sky.*

Wordsworth's vivid imagery and contemplative language invite readers to share in his profound emotional experience, showcasing how language can be both descriptive and reflective.

In the work of Maya Angelou, for instance, language becomes a vessel for profound truths and personal resilience. Her poem "*Still I Rise*" exemplifies how powerful language can be in conveying defiance and self-respect in the face of oppression.

> *You may shoot me with your words,*
> *You may cut me with your eyes,*
> *You may kill me with your hatefulness,*
> *But still, like air, I'll rise……*
> *Leaving behind nights of terror and fear*
> *I rise*
> *Into a daybreak that's wondrously clear*
> *I rise*
> *Bringing the gifts that my ancestors gave,*
> *I am the dream and the hope of the slave.*
> *I rise*
> *I rise*
> *I rise.*

Angelou's choice of words demonstrates poetry's capacity to express resilience and empowerment in a manner that resonates deeply with readers. The words, such as "trod" and "broken," carries a weight that underscores the poem's message of resistance and strength. The repeated phrase "I'll rise" serves as both a refrain and a declaration, emphasizing resilience and self-empowerment. Her use of language transforms personal struggle into a universal anthem of perseverance, illustrating poetry's capacity to express resilience and empowerment in a manner that resonates deeply with readers.

Similarly, in W.B. Yeats's "*The Second Coming*," the imagery and language evoke a sense of impending chaos and transformation:

> *Turning and turning in the widening gyre*
> *The falcon cannot hear the falconer.*
> *Things fall apart; the centre cannot hold;*
> *Mere anarchy is loosed upon the world,*
> *The blood-dimmed tide is loosed, and everywhere*
> *The ceremony of innocence is drowned;*

Yeats's use of vivid, unsettling images underscores the poem's themes of disintegration and rebirth, showcasing how language can shape the emotional and thematic impact of poetry.

5.2 Forms of Poetry

Poetry takes on many different shapes, and each form comes with its own set of rules, but rather than being limiting, these rules open up endless possibilities for creativity. From the structured elegance of a sonnet to the free-flowing nature of free verse, every form offers something unique. When you learn about these different poetic forms, you gain a deeper understanding of how language can be shaped, stretched, and molded to suit your ideas and emotions. Each form, whether strict or flexible, has a distinct way of helping you say what you want to say, in a way that feels right.

What makes poetic forms so powerful is their ability to help you bring out emotions in unique and impactful ways. The structure of a form like a sestina or a pantoum, with their intricate patterns of repetition, can add layers of meaning to your words, making them resonate more deeply with the reader. On the other hand, free verse allows for a raw, unrestricted flow of thought, where the lack of formal structure can reflect the unpredictability of emotions.

Sonnets: one of the most famous forms in English poetry, a sonnet is made up of 14 lines and usually follows a specific rhyme pattern and rhythm. The beauty of the sonnet is in its structure, which gives poets a framework to explore deep themes like love, beauty, and the passage of time. While the rules may seem strict, they actually offer a kind of freedom by giving poets a clear space to work within, allowing for profound emotional depth and thought.

With its carefully crafted form, the sonnet has been a favourite for poets like William Shakespeare, whose sonnets reflect on everything from the nature of love to the inevitable march of time. These poets use the form to express feelings that are timeless and universal, all within the tight framework of those 14 lines. It's a perfect example of how structure in poetry can enhance rather than limit creativity.

Shakespearean Sonnet

Shakespearean sonnet has a rhyming scheme of ABABCDCDEFEFGG and written in iambic pentameter. Take Sonnet 18 for example:

Shall I compare thee to a summer's day?
Thou art more lovely and more temperate:
Rough winds do shake the darling buds of May,
And summer's lease hath all too short a date:
Sometime too hot the eye of heaven shines,
And often is his gold complexion dimm'd;
And every fair from fair sometime declines,
By chance or nature's changing course untrimm'd;
But thy eternal summer shall not fade
Nor lose possession of that fair thou owest;
Nor shall Death brag thou wander'st in his shade,
When in eternal lines to time thou growest:

> *So long as men can breathe or eyes can see,*
> *So long lives this, and this gives life to thee.*

In this sonnet, Shakespeare uses the comparison of the beloved to a summer's day to explore themes of beauty and immortality. The structured rhyme scheme and meter enhance the poem's lyrical quality, allowing Shakespeare to express complex emotions within a confined space.

Haikus: Originating from Japan, haikus are known for their brevity and focus on nature. The haiku traditionally consists of three lines with a syllabic pattern of 5-7-5. Matsuo Bashō's "*The Old Pond*" is a classic example:

> *An old silent pond*
> *A frog jumps into the pond—*
> *Splash! Silence again.*

The simplicity of the haiku form captures a moment of tranquility, allowing the reader to experience the scene with clarity and immediacy. The brevity of the haiku invites a focus on the essence of a moment, reflecting a deep connection between the poet and the natural world.

Free Verse: In contrast to traditional forms, free verse allows for greater flexibility and freedom. Walt Whitman's *"Leaves of Grass"* is a seminal example of free verse poetry. Whitman's disregard for conventional rhyme and meter allows his poems to flow freely, mirroring the expansiveness of his themes. Consider this excerpt from *"Song of Myself"*:

> *I celebrate myself, and what I assume you shall assume,*
> *For every atom belonging to me as good belongs to you.*
> *I loafe and invite my soul,*
> *I lean and loafe at my ease observing a spear of summer grass.*

Whitman's use of free verse reflects his exploration of the self and the interconnectedness of all life. He employed free verse to explore the vastness of human experience and the American spirit. Whitman's disregard for conventional rhyme and meter allows his poems to flow freely, mirroring the expansiveness of his themes.

Villanelle: The villanelle is a 19-line form with a strict pattern of repetition and rhyme (ABA ABA ABA ABA ABA ABAA). The villanelle's structure demands a high level of repetition, which Dylan Thomas masterfully employs in his poem *"Do Not Go Gentle into That Good Night."* The poem opens with:

> *Do not go gentle into that good night,*
> *Old age should burn and rave at close of day;*
> *Rage, rage against the dying of the light.........*
> *And you, my father, there on the sad height,*
> *Curse, bless, me now with your fierce tears, I pray.*
> *Do not go gentle into that good night.*
> *Rage, rage against the dying of the light.*

Thomas repeats the first and third lines throughout the poem, creating a powerful refrain that underscores the poem's themes of defiance and resistance against death. The form's repetitive nature emphasizes the urgency of the speaker's plea, creating an emotionally charged atmosphere.

5.3. Techniques in Poetry

To bring poetry to life, poets use a range of techniques that add depth, emotion, and beauty to their words. These techniques are the building blocks of a powerful poem, shaping how a reader feels, imagines, and connects with the work. By mastering these tools, you can transform a simple collection of words into something that lingers in the reader's mind, making your poetry not just good, but unforgettable. A metaphor compares two unlike things to reveal a deeper truth, allowing readers to understand an emotion or idea in a new way. When Shakespeare wrote, *"All the world's a stage,"* he wasn't just talking about life; he was showing how our roles and actions are like those of actors in a play. Through metaphor, the poet creates connections that surprise and move the reader.

When a line of poetry runs over to the next without a pause, it creates momentum, pulling the reader forward. It's called enjambment. This technique breaks the usual rhythm and can build tension or surprise, keeping the reader engaged and making the poem more dynamic. Symbolism allows poets to infuse their work with deeper layers of meaning. A symbol can be an object, a person, or a situation that represents more than its literal meaning. For instance, a road in a poem might symbolize a life journey, as in Robert Frost's "*The Road Not Taken.*" Symbols give poetry richness, enabling a simple image to carry a wealth of ideas and emotions. The use of form and structure plays an important role in shaping a poem. Whether it's a carefully structured sonnet or a free-flowing open verse, the way a poem is built affects its rhythm, mood, and impact. Knowing when to follow tradition and when to break away from it can make all the difference in a poem's emotional power.

Imagery: One key technique is imagery, which uses vivid descriptions to create mental pictures and provide sensory experiences. With imagery, a poet paints a scene or emotion so clearly that the reader can see, hear, smell, or even feel it. Whether it's the warmth of the sun in a summer field or the cold bite of winter wind, imagery helps bring the poem's world to life. As Ezra Pound famously said, "*Go in fear of abstractions,*" (Pound 5) meaning that concrete images — not abstract ideas — make poetry come alive.

In the works of Indian poet Rabindranath Tagore, such as "*Where the Mind Is Without Fear,*" the imagery evokes a vision of a liberated, enlightened world:

Where the mind is without fear and the head is held high;
Where knowledge is free;
Where the world has not been broken up into fragments
By narrow domestic walls;
Where words come out from the depth of truth;
Where tireless striving stretches its arms towards perfection;
Where the clear stream of reason has not lost its way
Into the dreary desert sand of dead habit;
Where the mind is led forward by thee
Into ever-widening thought and action—
Into that heaven of freedom, my Father, let my country awake.

Tagore's use of imagery here paints a picture of a utopian vision where freedom and enlightenment prevail. His descriptive language creates a powerful contrast between the ideal and the real, inviting readers to envision a world of possibility and hope.

Similarly, African poet Chinua Achebe's "*Refugee Mother and Child*" uses striking imagery to evoke the harsh realities faced by refugees, making the reader feel the depth of the characters' suffering and resilience.

No Madonna and Child could touch
That picture of a mother's tenderness
For a son she soon would have to forget.
The air was heavy with odours of diarrhea
Of intestinal worm, and malaria:
And so the mother did what heroes do,
As she had done in the days of the great drought,
The great drought of 1984.

Achebe's imagery brings to life the dire conditions faced by refugees and the unyielding love of a mother. His vivid descriptions not only paint a clear picture of the situation but also elicit an emotional response from the reader, deepening the impact of the poem.

Rhyme: The use of rhyme can create musicality and reinforce thematic connections. It involves the repetition of similar sounds, typically at the end of lines, and can contribute to a poem's rhythm and aesthetic appeal. Sound in poetry is created through alliteration, assonance, or rhyme. These techniques control the rhythm and flow of a poem, making the words feel musical and pleasing to the ear. Alliteration, the repetition of consonant sounds (like in "wild winds whip"), gives the poem a rhythmic quality. Similarly, assonance, the repetition of vowel sounds, can soften or sharpen a line depending on the effect the poet wants to achieve. Sound patterns create a mood, enhance meaning, and make the poem more memorable.

Take for example, Edgar Allan Poe's poem "*The Raven*," in which the repetition of the rhyme scheme enhances the poem's melancholic and eerie atmosphere. For instance:

> *Once upon a midnight dreary, while I pondered, weak and weary,*
> *Over many a quaint and curious volume of forgotten lore—*
> *While I nodded, nearly napping, suddenly there came a tapping,*
> *As of some one gently rapping, rapping at my chamber door.*
> *"'Tis some visitor," I muttered, "tapping at my chamber door—*
> *Only this and nothing more."*

Poe's use of the rhyme scheme—particularly the repeated refrain "Nevermore"—creates a haunting rhythm that underscores the poem's themes of loss and despair. The rhyme contributes to the poem's musical quality, enhancing its emotional resonance.

Meter: In Alfred Lord Tennyson's "*The Charge of the Light Brigade*," the use of dactylic meter brings a sense of urgency and movement to the poem. The opening lines illustrate this:

> *Half a league, half a league,*
> *Half a league onward,*
> *All in the valley of Death*
> *Rode the six hundred.*

Each line follows a dactylic rhythm, where the pattern of one stressed syllable followed by two unstressed syllables (DUM-da-da) mimics the sound of galloping horses. This rhythm not only drives the poem forward but also mirrors the relentless advance of the soldiers into battle, capturing the intensity and pace of the charge.

5.4. Finding Your Voice

Your unique voice is the essence of your poetry. It reflects your personal style, perspective, and experiences, distinguishing your work from that of others. Discovering and cultivating your voice involves exploring your individual experiences and perspectives and allowing them to shape your poetic expression. Canadian poet Margaret Atwood's work often blends personal narrative with broader social commentary, reflecting her distinctive voice and perspective. Her poetry and prose are marked by a deep engagement with themes of identity, gender, and societal issues. Finding your voice involves exploring your individual experiences and perspectives and allowing them to shape your poetic expression.

Emotions of the poet: Poetry is most powerful when it conveys genuine emotion. Authenticity in emotion can resonate with readers on a profound level, allowing them to connect with your work more deeply. In *"The Love Song of J. Alfred Prufrock,"* T.S. Eliot uses stream-of-consciousness and fragmented imagery to capture the inner turmoil and existential anxiety of the protagonist.

> *Let us go then, you and I,*
> *When the evening is spread out against the sky*
> *Like a patient etherized upon a table;*
> *Let us go, through certain half-deserted streets,*
> *The muttering retreats*
> *Of restless nights in one-night cheap hotels*
> *And sawdust restaurants with oyster-shells:*

Eliot's use of disjointed imagery and introspective language reflects Prufrock's inner conflict and sense of alienation. By embracing and articulating his emotional complexity, Eliot creates a resonant and evocative portrayal of modern existential angst.

Creating Resonance: Resonance in poetry occurs when the poem strikes a chord with the reader, evoking a personal response or reflection. A poem that resonates has the power to connect with readers on an emotional level, making the experience of reading it both personal and profound. Indian poet Kamala Das's *"My Mother at Sixty-Six"* resonates deeply through its exploration of aging and familial love.

> *Driving from my parents' home*
> *to Cochin last Friday morning,*
> *I saw my mother beside me,*
> *doze, open-mouthed, her face*
> *ashen like that of a corpse*
> *and realized with pain*
> *that she was as old as she looked.*

Das's touching reflection on her mother's aging and the inevitability of time creates a powerful emotional connection with the reader. The poem's exploration of universal themes of family and aging invites readers to reflect on their own relationships and experiences.

Revising Thoughtfully: Revision is crucial for making an impactful poem. Poets often refine their work multiple times to achieve the desired effect, ensuring that each word and line contributes to the overall message and emotional resonance. The original draft should be revised multiple times by refining its language and structure to capture the poem's themes more precisely.

5.5. How to Write a Compelling Poem

Writing a compelling poem involves a combination of creativity, technique, and revision. Writing a compelling poem is an art form that invites both emotion and imagination. The journey of writing poetry is not just about the words you choose; it's about exploring the rhythm, imagery, and emotions that make your voice unique. Embracing the creative process can lead to unexpected discoveries and profound connections, both for you as a writer and for your readers.

Start with a Strong Image or Idea: Begin with a powerful image, emotion, or concept that you want to explore. Look at these opening lines of W.B. Yeats's "*The Second Coming*"

Turning and turning in the widening gyre
The falcon cannot hear the falconer;
Things fall apart; the centre cannot hold;
Mere anarchy is loosed upon the world,

These lines immediately draw the reader in with striking imagery and a sense of impending change. Start with an image or emotion that will take your reader into your poem immediately.

Use Precise Language: Choose your words carefully to convey the intended emotion or imagery. Precision in language helps to create vivid pictures and evoke strong feelings. Here's an example of a poem titled *Red Wheelbarrow* by William Carlos William:

so much depends
upon
a red wheel
barrow
glazed with rain
water
beside the white
chickens

The poet uses minimal language, creating an impact with just a few lines. It demonstrates that simplicity can convey deep significance. The vivid image of the "red wheelbarrow" and "white chickens" captures a specific scene with clarity. The colour contrast enhances the visual impact, making the reader visualize the scene distinctly. The enjambment flows smoothly, guiding the reader through the imagery. The opening line, "so much depends," elevates the mundane to something profound, suggesting that ordinary objects can hold significant meaning. This invites readers to reflect on their own experiences and the importance of simple things in life.

Experiment with Form and Structure: Experiment with different forms and structures to find the best fit for your poem. Whether you choose a traditional form or free verse, ensure that the structure enhances your poem's content and message.

Revise and Refine: Revise your poem to improve clarity, rhythm, and emotional impact. Pay attention to how each word contributes to the overall effect. Canadian poet Leonard Cohen famously said, "*Poetry is just the evidence of life. If your life is burning well, poetry is just the ash.*" Cohen, 287) Use revision to refine your poetic expression.

Seek Feedback: Share your poem with others to gain different perspectives. Feedback can provide valuable insights into how your poem resonates with readers and suggest areas for improvement. Before you aim for larger feedback from the readers, use beta readers to get the feedback first which can help improve work before you publish.

Reflect and Revise: Reflect on the feedback and make necessary revisions. The process of refinement is essential for transforming a good poem into a compelling and impactful work of art. Each revision brings you closer to achieving the poem's intended effect, allowing you to refine your expression to its essence.

Writing Prompt: Random Word Poetry

Choose a Book: Select a book that you find interesting. This could be a novel, a collection of poetry, or a non-fiction book.

Select Words: Open the book to random pages and select five to six words from each page. Make sure to avoid articles (a, an, the) and helping verbs (is, was, have) while selecting your words.

Create a Word Pool: Make sure the words are selected randomly like line five word six. Stick to the same pattern while selecting words. Compile all the words you've collected into a list.

Write Your Poem: Using the words from your list, write a poem. You can use articles and helping verbs as needed to create grammatical structure, and you can change the form of the verbs to fit the poem's rhythm and flow.

Edit and Refine: Once you've drafted your poem, revise it for clarity, coherence, and poetic impact. Pay attention to how the chosen words interact and create imagery or emotion.

References

Achebe, Chinua. "Refugee Mother and Child." *Collected Poems*, Anchor Books, 2004.

Angelou, Maya. "Still I Rise." *And Still I Rise: A Book of Poems*, Random House, 1978.

Auden, W. H. "The Poet & the City." *The Dyer's Hand and Other Essays*, Random House, 1962, p. 27.

Bashō, Matsuo. "The Old Pond." Translated by Sam Hamill, *The Sound of Water: Haiku by Bashō, Buson, Issa, and Other Poets*, Shambhala Publications, 2000.

Cohen, Leonard. Interview by BBC Radio 1. *Leonard Cohen: Interviews and Encounters*, edited by Jeff Burger, Chicago Review Press, 2014, p. 287.

Dickinson, Emily. *The Letters of Emily Dickinson*. Edited by Thomas H. Johnson, Harvard University Press, 1958.

Eliot, T. S. "Dante." *Selected Prose of T. S. Eliot*, edited by Frank Kermode, Harcourt, 1975, p. 206.

Eliot, T. S. "The Love Song of J. Alfred Prufrock." *Prufrock and Other Observations*, The Egoist Ltd., 1917.

Frost, Robert. "The Figure a Poem Makes." *Collected Poems, Prose, and Plays*, edited by Richard Poirier and Mark Richardson, Library of America, 1955, p. 776.

Frost, Robert. "The Road Not Taken." *Mountain Interval*, Henry Holt and Company, 1916.

Poe, Edgar Allan. "The Raven." *The Raven and Other Poems*, Wiley and Putnam, 1845.

Pound, Ezra. "A Retrospect." *Literary Essays of Ezra Pound*, edited by T. S. Eliot, New Directions, 1954, p. 5.

Tagore, Rabindranath. "Where the Mind is Without Fear." *Gitanjali*, translated by the author, Macmillan, 1912.

Tennyson, Alfred, Lord. "The Charge of the Light Brigade." *Maud, and Other Poems*, Edward Moxon, 1855.

Thomas, Dylan. "Do Not Go Gentle into That Good Night." *In Country Sleep and Other Poems*, New Directions, 1952.

Whitman, Walt. "Song of Myself." *Leaves of Grass*, 1855.

Williams, William Carlos. "The Red Wheelbarrow." *Spring and All*, Contact Publishing Co., 1923.

Wordsworth, William. "Lines Composed a Few Miles Above Tintern Abbey." *Lyrical Ballads*, J. & A. Arch, 1798.

Wordsworth, William. "Preface to Lyrical Ballads." *Lyrical Ballads*, Longman and Rees, 1802.

Yeats, W. B. "The Second Coming." *The Dial*, Nov. 1920.

Chapter 6

Writing Fiction

Fiction is the art of creating imagined worlds where not just characters but also plotline, dialogue and sometimes setting as well are invented into narratives. Even when all of these are invented and are imaginary, they still resonate with readers. Whether it's through short stories, novellas, or sprawling novels, writing fiction allows writers to explore the human condition, confront complex ideas, and build universes that linger in the reader's mind. This chapter will explore the key elements

> Fiction is such a world of freedom. It's wonderful. If you want someone to fly, they can fly."
>
> _Alice Walker

of fiction writing, from crafting compelling narratives to building immersive worlds, the importance of narrative voice, and the role of conflict and motivation in character development. It will also take examples from renowned books to deepen our understanding of what makes fiction so powerful.

6.1. Creating Compelling Narratives

At the heart of any work of fiction is its narrative—the unfolding story that holds the reader's attention from beginning to end. A compelling narrative is more than just a sequence of events; it is the result of intentional structure, pacing, and character development. As E.M. Forster famously explained in *Aspects of the Novel*, "*The king died, and then the queen died is a story. The king died, and then the queen died of grief is a plot.*" Foster, 87) This distinction reminds us that the why behind events is crucial to creating a meaningful and engaging story.

Structure and Plot

Most compelling narratives follow a structure that keeps the reader invested in the unfolding story. Whether it's Aristotle's Three-Act Structure or Freytag's Pyramid, structure helps writers shape the rise and fall of tension. Freytag's Pyramid, for example, divides a story into exposition, rising action, climax, falling action, and denouement, providing a clear path for the narrative's emotional arc. Robert McKee emphasizes, "*Structure is the selection of events from the characters' life stories that is composed into a strategic sequence to arouse specific emotions and to express a specific view of life.*" (McKee 31)

Many modern novels, from Chimamanda Ngozi Adichie's *Half of a Yellow Sun* to Ian McEwan's *Atonement*, use these structural elements to frame complex narratives, blending personal and political conflict with moments of intense emotional impact. The narrative thread pulls the reader along, making them care about what happens next while revealing deeper truths about the characters and the world they inhabit.

Conflict and Stakes

Central to a compelling narrative is conflict, which drives the plot forward and forces characters to evolve. Conflict can be internal, like the psychological struggles of Virginia Woolf's *Mrs. Dalloway*, where Clarissa Dalloway grapples with her past choices and the fleeting nature of life. It can also be external, as seen in George Orwell's *1984*, where Winston Smith confronts a totalitarian regime, or in Man Booker Prize-winner Arundhati Roy's *The God of Small Things*, which explores familial and societal conflicts in the context of caste and forbidden love in India.

For a narrative to be compelling, the stakes must feel significant. The reader should feel that the characters' decisions and actions have real consequences, as this generates emotional investment. As James Scott Bell notes in *Plot & Structure*, "*Your character must want something—something vital. And it must be difficult to get.*" (Bell 34) Whether it's the survival of a relationship, a personal revelation, or even the fate of the world, stakes keep the reader engaged and emotionally connected to the characters.

6.2. Building Worlds: Setting and Atmosphere

The setting of a work of fiction is far more than just a backdrop. It shapes the mood, influences the characters, and often becomes a character in itself. From the moody streets of Charles Dickens's *Bleak House* to the vast, fantastical worlds of J.R.R. Tolkien's *The Lord of the Rings*, a well-crafted setting immerses readers and enhances the narrative's emotional texture.

Creating Vivid Worlds

To create a world that feels real, writers need to pay attention to detail. In *On Writing*, Stephen King emphasizes the importance of grounding even fantastical worlds in reality. "*The best fiction,*" he writes, "*seems to be propelled by an agenda of emotional honesty.*" (King 128) Whether your setting is a quiet suburban town or a dystopian future, the key is to make the world internally consistent and believable.

A great example of world-building can be seen in Margaret Atwood's *The Handmaid's Tale*. Atwood constructs a chilling dystopia, the Republic of Gilead, with its own rules, language, and hierarchy. Every detail, from the color-coded dresses to the political slogans, serves to deepen the oppressive atmosphere of the novel. Similarly, African writer Chinua Achebe's *Things Fall Apart* brings to life the pre-colonial village of Umuofia, painting a vivid picture of its customs, rituals, and conflicts with colonial forces.

Atmosphere and Mood

Atmosphere is a tool that enhances the reader's emotional engagement with the story. It can be shaped through the sensory details of the setting, the weather, or the emotional tone of the scenes. In Thomas Hardy's *Tess of the d'Urbervilles*, for example, the landscape and the changing seasons mirror Tess's inner turmoil and external challenges. The dark, brooding atmosphere of Hardy's rural settings reflects the novel's tragic themes.

On the other hand, Indian writer Arundhati Roy's *The Ministry of Utmost Happiness*, the atmosphere of modern Delhi, with its political unrest and sprawling cityscapes, adds layers of tension to the personal stories of the characters. Atmosphere in fiction often serves as a reflection of the emotional landscape of the characters, enhancing the thematic depth of the narrative.

6.3. Narrative Voice in Fiction

One of the most distinctive elements of any work of fiction is its narrative voice. The narrative voice not only determines the point of view but also shapes the reader's relationship with the story and characters.

First-Person Narration

First-person narration provides an intimate glimpse into the thoughts and emotions of the narrator, offering a personal connection to the narrative. J.D. Salinger, in his book *The Catcher in the Rye* uses first-person narration that creates a raw, unfiltered window into Holden Caulfield's adolescent mind. The voice is distinctively Holden's; sarcastic, troubled, and introspective—giving readers direct access to his inner world.

Similarly, the character of Janie Crawford in *Their Eyes Were Watching God* by African-American writer Zora Neale Hurston, has a voice which is a blend of personal reflection and dialect, immersing the reader in her journey of self-discovery. Hurston's use of first-person narration helps to convey Janie's inner strength and resilience, making her voice a powerful force in the narrative.

In first person narration, the story is filtered through the narrator's personal experiences and biases, providing a unique lens on events. Readers often feel more involved in the story, as they experience events directly through the narrator's eyes.

Third-Person Limited and Omniscient Narration

Third-person narration can either be limited (focused on one character's perspective) or omniscient (able to explore multiple characters' thoughts). In *Pride and Prejudice*, Jane Austen employs a third-person omniscient narrator, allowing the reader to see the thoughts and motivations of various characters, from Elizabeth Bennet's sharp wit to Mr. Darcy's internal conflicts. Similarly, in Canadian writer Margaret Atwood's *The Blind Assassin*, the third-person omniscient narrative allows for the seamless interweaving of past and present, reality and fiction, creating a richly layered story that deepens the reader's understanding of the characters and the world they inhabit.

Third person narration allows for a broader exploration of the plot and setting, making it easier to convey complex narratives involving multiple characters. It can switch between characters and provide different viewpoints, enhancing the depth of the story.

Both first person and third person narration offer distinct advantages in shaping how a story is perceived. While first-person uses "I" or "we," third-person uses "he," "she," "they," or "it." First-person offers direct insight into one character's mind, while third-person can provide a wider range of perspectives. In first-person, the narrator's reliability can be questionable, whereas third-person can offer a more objective overview. Choosing between these perspectives affects the emotional impact and complexity of the narrative, guiding how readers engage with the story.

6.4. Short Stories, Novellas, and Novels: Techniques and Approaches

Different forms of fiction—short stories, novellas, and novels—require distinct techniques and approaches to storytelling. Each format offers unique opportunities for experimentation and depth, shaping how narratives unfold and resonate with readers. While all forms aim to evoke emotion and convey themes, their structural differences necessitate varied methods of engagement.

Short stories, with their concise nature, demand precision and focus, often connecting complex ideas into a single moment or impactful twist. This brevity challenges writers to craft narratives that are rich in imagery and emotion within a limited space. Conversely, novellas allow for a middle ground, offering more room for character development and plot complexity while still retaining a streamlined narrative. Novels, on the other hand, provide an expansive canvas, enabling intricate world-building and multifaceted character arcs. This diverse landscape of fiction invites writers to explore their creativity and experiment with different storytelling techniques.

6.4.1. Writing Short Stories

Short stories condense a narrative into a brief yet impactful form. In her book *Mystery and Manners,* writer Flannery O'Connor explained, *"The short story doesn't take long to read, but it should make a lasting impression."* (O'Connor 93) Short stories often focus on a single moment, character, or conflict, making every word count. Unlike novels, which can explore a wide range of themes and events, short stories often hone in on one central idea, making every word count. Jhumpa Lahiri's *Interpreter of Maladies*, a collection of short stories, exemplifies how this form can explore themes of displacement, cultural identity, and human relationships with depth and nuance in just a few pages.

Short stories also provide a unique space for experimentation with structure, voice, and time. Writers are free to play with narrative techniques that may not work as well in a longer format. For example, Chimamanda Ngozi Adichie's *The Thing Around Your Neck* is a collection that uses short stories to explore complex emotional landscapes, often highlighting the tension between tradition and modernity, cultural identity, and immigration. In these stories, Adichie experiments with perspectives and narrative forms, offering glimpses into the lives of her characters that feel both intimate and expansive. Her stories showcase how the brevity of the short story form can be used to create sharp, lasting impressions that linger long after the story is over.

Indian short stories have also made a significant contribution to this form of storytelling. R.K. Narayan, for example, is well known for his collection *Malgudi Days*, which brings to life the fictional town of Malgudi, capturing the essence of Indian rural life in a series of short, yet impactful stories. Narayan's writing is simple but evocative, portraying ordinary characters and everyday situations in a way that reveals deeper truths about human nature, society, and culture. His short stories, often humorous and touching, reflect the complexities of Indian life while also highlighting universal themes of love, loss, and aspiration. Another notable Indian short story writer is Saadat Hasan Manto, whose works like *Toba Tek Singh* takes you to the times of partition of India, showcasing the deep emotional and psychological scars left by this traumatic event. His short stories, though concise, pack a punch, addressing themes of identity, displacement, and the absurdities of political borders.

6.4.2. Writing Novellas

The novella is a unique type of storytelling that sits between a short story and a full-length novel. It allows writers to develop characters and themes in more depth than a short story but without the length and complexity of a novel. This makes the novella a powerful tool for telling focused, impactful stories that can explore deep ideas and emotions without being overwhelming.

Another powerful novella is George Orwell's *Animal Farm*. This story, written as an allegory, uses farm animals to represent the events leading up to the Russian Revolution and the rise of totalitarianism. The novella's concise form helps Orwell focus on the key themes of power, corruption, and the betrayal of ideals. By using animals to tell this story, Orwell simplifies complex political ideas while still delivering a strong and impactful message about the dangers of absolute power. Even though *Animal Farm* is short, it remains one of the most famous and influential works of political fiction.

John Steinbeck's *Of Mice and Men* is another example of how the novella can deliver a strong emotional impact. The story of George and Lennie, two migrant workers during the Great Depression, captures themes of friendship, loneliness, and shattered dreams. Steinbeck's novella uses its short length to focus on the intense bond between the two men and the harsh reality of the world they live in, leaving readers with a deep emotional experience.

The novella's strength lies in its ability to tell a complete, meaningful story in a compact form. Writers can focus on a single narrative, theme, or character arc, allowing for an in-depth exploration of ideas without the need for long chapters or complex plots. Readers, in turn, benefit from the novella's ability to deliver a rich, layered story in a shorter amount of time.

6.4.3. Writing Novels

The novel, with its length and complexity, allows for deep exploration of character, setting, and plot. As E.M. Forster points out in *Aspects of the Novel*, *"The novel tells a story."* The longer form of the novel gives writers room to develop subplots, create intricate character arcs, and build immersive worlds. In Salman Rushdie's *Midnight's Children*, the expansive narrative spans generations, weaving historical events with personal stories, blending magical realism with political commentary.

Novels offer the opportunity to dive deeply into the human condition, exploring the intersection of personal and societal forces. In *Beloved* by Toni Morrison, the novel's sprawling narrative not only delves into the legacy of slavery but also investigates the haunting, emotional landscape of trauma and memory. Through Morrison's masterful use of language, history, and symbolism, the novel becomes a vehicle for exploring both the personal and collective past. Writing a novel requires sustained attention to character development, world-building, and plot progression.

6.5. Other Elements of Writing Fiction

Beyond plot, setting, and narrative voice, there are other crucial elements to consider when writing fiction, like, Symbolism and Theme, Dialogue and Character Interaction, Pacing and Tension.

Symbolism and Theme: Symbolism in fiction acts as a subtle yet profound narrative device, enriching themes and deepening a story's emotional and intellectual impact. By embedding objects, settings, or recurring motifs with layered meaning, writers can convey complex ideas without explicit exposition. In William Golding's *Lord of the Flies*, the conch shell is used as a powerful emblem of order and democracy. When the boys first gather, the conch grants its holder the right to speak, symbolizing civilized discourse. However, as the story progresses and the conch is shattered, its destruction marks the collapse of rationality, foreshadowing the boys' descent into primal violence. This deliberate use of symbolism reinforces Golding's exploration of human nature and the fragility of societal structures.

Symbolism can take many forms—a recurring color, a weather pattern, or even a silent object charged with meaning. In *To Kill a Mockingbird*, Harper Lee uses the mockingbird as a symbol of innocence and injustice, while in *1984*, George Orwell's omnipresent telescreens embody oppressive surveillance. When crafted effectively, symbols resonate with readers, allowing themes to linger long after the final page.

Themes are the underlying messages or central ideas of a story. Whether it's love, identity, freedom, or justice, a strong theme ties together the narrative threads and gives the story its emotional and intellectual core. In her book *Steering the Craft*, Ursula K. Le Guin suggests, "*A story's theme arises naturally from its subject and the choices the characters make.*" (Le Guin 47)

Dialogue and Character Interaction: Dialogue is one of the most dynamic tools in fiction, serving multiple purposes—revealing personality, advancing the plot, and creating tension—all while mimicking the rhythms of real speech. However, great dialogue does more than convey information; it thrives on subtext, the unspoken emotions and motivations beneath the words. A character might say, "Fine, do whatever you want," while their clenched jaw and defensive posture communicate resentment or helplessness. This layering of meaning makes exchanges feel authentic and charged with conflict or desire.

Beyond dialogue, character interactions—how individuals relate, clash, or connect—shape the emotional core of a story. Relationships can drive the narrative, whether through the bitter rivalry between Sherlock Holmes and Moriarty, or the slow-burning romance between Elizabeth Bennet and Mr. Darcy in *Pride and Prejudice*. Jane Austen's sharp, witty exchanges don't just entertain; they expose class tensions, personal biases, and evolving affections.

Mastering dialogue and character interaction means understanding that every conversation is a negotiation of power, desire, or fear. Whether through heated arguments, loaded pauses, or unspoken understandings, these elements make fictional relationships feel alive.

Pacing and Tension: Pacing is the rhythm of your story—how fast or slow the events unfold. Think of it like a rollercoaster: some stories race forward with quick twists while others take their time, letting you sink into the characters' emotions. Fast pacing keeps readers hooked with action, short scenes, and cliffhangers. Mystery and thriller novels, like *Gone Girl* by Gillian Flynn, use fast pacing to make the reader eager to turn the page. Slow pacing allows for deeper character development and rich descriptions. Books like *The Book Thief* by Markus Zusak take time to explore emotions and relationships, making the story feel more real and meaningful.

Tension is what makes readers worry about what happens next. It can come from external tension—danger, conflicts, or high-stakes problems. Internal tension comes from a character's fears, secrets, or moral struggles. A great story balances both pacing and tension.

6.6. Writing Fiction Across Cultures

Fiction is a universal art form, and writers from around the world bring unique perspectives and cultural insights to their work. Indian writer Salman Rushdie's *Midnight's Children* explores the history of post-colonial India through magical realism, blending

> "Writing fiction is the act of weaving a series of lies to arrive at a greater truth."
>
> _Khaled Hosseini

the personal and political in a deeply textured narrative. Similarly, Nigerian author Chimamanda Ngozi Adichie's *Half of a Yellow Sun* uses the Nigerian Civil War as a backdrop for a moving exploration of love, loss, and identity.

Canadian writer Alice Munro, known for her short stories, brings the subtle shades of human relationships to life with precision and grace. In her collection *Dear Life*, Munro's stories capture the quiet, everyday moments that shape lives, demonstrating how fiction can find power in the ordinary. Each of these writers illustrates how fiction can transcend borders, offering readers a window into lives, cultures, and worlds far beyond their own.

6.7. Crafting Timeless Fiction

Writing great fiction takes work, but when you understand the key ingredients, you can create stories that stay with readers long after they finish. To write well, as a writer, consider and keep the following in mind:

1. Be Real: The best stories come from truth—even if they're about dragons or futuristic worlds. Write about what matters to you, and your passion will pull readers in. As Kurt Vonnegut said, *"Write to please just one person. If you open a window and make love to the world, so to speak, your story will get pneumonia."* (Vonnegut 9)

2. Make It Messy (In a Good Way!): Perfect characters and simple "good vs. evil" plots are forgettable. What makes stories exciting? Flaws, tough choices, and surprises. Katniss in *The Hunger Games* isn't just brave—she's stubborn, distrustful, and sometimes reckless. In *The Fault in Our Stars*, Hazel and Augustus joke about cancer while grappling with love and fear. Don't be afraid of complicated emotions or endings that aren't neatly tied up. Real life isn't like that!

3. Rewrite, Rewrite, Rewrite: Your first draft is just you telling yourself the story. The real magic happens when you edit. Cut boring parts, make dialogue sharper, flesh out weak scenes. J.K. Rowling rewrote Harry Potter chapters dozens of times. As author Neil Gaiman says, *"The process of writing can be magical. Mostly it's a process of putting one word after another until you're done. Then doing it again."* (Gaiman 32)

Writing Prompts

A Mysterious Gift
Write a story where a character receives a package with no return address, containing an item that holds significant meaning from a pivotal moment in their past. How does this item affect their current life, and what revelations or consequences arise from it?

Echoes from Tomorrow
Begin a story with a character discovering a newspaper article from the future that details an event they are about to experience. How does the knowledge of this future event influence their decisions and

The Forgotten Journal
Write about a character who finds a diary they wrote as a child, but with entries that seem to predict future events. As they read through it, they realize they are about to face one of the predicted events and must confront their past self's

A Stranger's Request
Start a story with a character being approached by a stranger who claims to be from an alternate reality or timeline, seeking their help to prevent a disaster that only they can stop.

The Enchanted Pen
Write about a writer who discovers an old pen that allows them to write stories that come to life. As their fictional creations begin to interfere with their real life, they must find a way to balance imagination and reality.

The Time-Turner's Dilemma
Begin with a character finding an antique time-turner or hourglass that allows them to revisit past moments in their life. They must decide whether to change a significant event or accept the consequences of their choices.

References

Adichie, Chimamanda Ngozi. *The Thing Around Your Neck*. Alfred A. Knopf, 2009.

Adichie, Chimamanda Ngozi. *Half of a Yellow Sun*. Alfred A. Knopf, 2006.

Bell, James Scott. *Plot & Structure: Techniques and Exercises for Crafting a Plot That Grips Readers from Start to Finish*. Writer's Digest Books, 2004, p. 34.

Forster, E. M. *Aspects of the Novel*. Edited by Oliver Stallybrass, Penguin Classics, 2005, p. 87.

Gaiman, Neil. *Art Matters: Because Your Imagination Can Change the World*. Illustrated by Chris Riddell, HarperCollins, 2018, p. 32.

Hardy, Thomas. *Tess of the d'Urbervilles*. Penguin Classics, 2003.

Hurston, Zora Neale. *Their Eyes Were Watching God*. Harper Perennial Modern Classics, 2006.

King, Stephen. *On Writing: A Memoir of the Craft*. Scribner, 2000, p. 128.

Le Guin, Ursula K. *Steering the Craft: A Twenty-First-Century Guide to Sailing the Sea of Story*. Mariner Books, 2015, p. 47.

McEwan, Ian. *Atonement*. Jonathan Cape, 2001.

McKee, Robert. *Story: Substance, Structure, Style, and the Principles of Screenwriting*. HarperCollins, 1997, p. 31.

Narayan, R. K. *Malgudi Days*. Indian Thought Publications, 1943.

O'Connor, Flannery. *Mystery and Manners: Occasional Prose*. Edited by Sally and Robert Fitzgerald, Farrar, Straus and Giroux, 1969, p. 93.

Orwell, George. *Animal Farm*. Secker and Warburg, 1945.

Roy, Arundhati. *The Ministry of Utmost Happiness*. Penguin Random House India, 2017.

Salinger, J. D. *The Catcher in the Rye*. Little, Brown and Company, 1951.

Scott, Paul. *The Blind Assassin*. McClelland and Stewart, 2000.

Vonnegut, Kurt. *Bagombo Snuff Box: Uncollected Short Fiction*. G.P. Putnam's Sons, 1999, p. 9.

Chapter 7

Writing Non-Fiction

Many people mistakenly believe nonfiction is just about reporting facts, but the best nonfiction reads like a gripping novel—it just happens to be true. Creative nonfiction is where journalism meets storytelling, blending real-world accuracy with the emotional power of great fiction. Whether you're writing a memoir, biography,

> "Creative nonfiction writers do not make things up; they make ideas and information that already exist more interesting and often more accessible."
>
> _Lee Gutkind

investigative piece, or personal essay, your goal is the same: to make facts as compelling as fiction while staying 100% true to reality.

7.1 The Art of Telling True Stories

The essence of non-fiction writing is to present reality in a way that captivates readers. The challenge lies in making factual information engaging without compromising truthfulness. John McPhee in *Draft No. 4* notes, "*The purpose of non-fiction is to convert factual material into something memorable – to take the dry bones of information and breathe life into them. You can't do this by merely piling up facts. You need to shape them, arrange them and infuse them with narrative energy so they lodge in the reader's mind.*" (McPhee 157) This transformation of facts into compelling narratives involves a blend of storytelling techniques and journalistic rigor.

The misconception that nonfiction is merely informational—devoid of creativity—ignores the genre's richest works: memoirs that read like novels, biographies that unfold like thrillers, and essays that blend personal confession with cultural critique. The power of creative nonfiction lies in its ability to:

1. Make the Personal Universal: A well-told true story doesn't just recount events; it connects them to larger human experiences. *When Breath Becomes Air* (Paul Kalanithi) transcends one man's battle with cancer to explore mortality, purpose, and what makes life meaningful.

2. Clarify Complexity: Through narrative, writers can unpack dense subjects (science, history, politics) in ways that engage rather than lecture. *The Devil in the White City* (Erik Larson) intertwines architectural history with a serial killer's crimes, turning urban planning into a suspense story.

3. Preserve and Reinterpret Truth: Memory is fallible, history is contested, and perspective shapes reality. Creative nonfiction acknowledges this while striving for honesty. *The Liars' Club* (Mary Karr) grapples with the slippery nature of childhood memory, admitting gaps while reconstructing her past with vivid scenes.

Key Elements:

1. Narrative Structure: Unlike fiction, where plot can be invented, creative nonfiction requires structuring existing events into a coherent, compelling arc. Even when writing about real events, you need a clear structure to keep readers hooked. You need to choose whether to use chronological order, Flashbacks or Thematic organisation. Even if readers know the outcome (e.g., historical events), the how and why can remain gripping.

2. Character Development: In fiction, characters are crafted; in nonfiction, they're revealed. Characters in nonfiction are actual people, but they still need dimension. Readers should understand their motives, flaws, and contradictions. Therefore, it demands deep research and empathy and no one-dimensional portrayals. Details and specificity bring real people to life: a subject's catchphrase, a telling object, an incongruous habit.

3. Balancing Truth and Storytelling: Creative nonfiction isn't about embellishing—it's about framing reality in a way that resonates.

Do: Use vivid scenes (e.g., *In Cold Blood* by Truman Capote reconstructs key moments like a novel).

Don't: Invent conversations or alter facts. If you're unsure about a detail, say so (e.g., "She likely felt..." instead of "She thought...").

4. Voice & Style: Your perspective matters! Voice in creative nonfiction isn't just about flair—it's about perspective. A personal, engaging voice can make even niche topics fascinating. A humorous voice can disarm readers about tough topics, while a lyrical voice can elevate the mundane.

<u>**Exercises:**</u>

1.The "Fact-to-Scene" Challenge: Take a dry news article and rewrite it as a narrative scene. Add sensory details (smells, sounds) and inner monologue based only on research.

2. Perspective Switch: Write about a personal memory from someone else's viewpoint (a family member, a bystander). This reveals biases in your own storytelling.

3. Ethics Roleplay: Journalists often face dilemmas: "Your subject admits to lying earlier. Do you revise your draft?" Debate these scenarios with peers.

7.2. Memoirs and Personal Essays

Creative nonfiction includes diverse forms like memoirs (personal narratives exploring identity and memory) and personal essays (reflective pieces connecting individual experiences to universal themes). Writers employ vivid imagery, character development, and scene construction to transform real events into engaging narratives while maintaining journalistic integrity. By blending storytelling with truth-telling, creative nonfiction illuminates human experiences with both emotional resonance and intellectual depth.

Memoirs:

Memoirs are a special kind of writing that give readers a glimpse into the author's personal experiences and thoughts. They aren't just about telling life events, but about exploring emotions, growth, and lessons learned. Mary Karr in her book *The Art of Memoir* says, "*A memoir's purpose is to convey a deeply felt sense of personal truth and emotional resonance.*" (Karr 6) This truth allows readers to connect with the author's journey and find parts of themselves in the story.

Good memoirs often blend personal stories with bigger ideas, making them relatable. For instance, Tara Westover's *Educated* doesn't just focus on her unique childhood away from traditional schooling but also touches on themes like family, identity, and the importance of education. This mix of the personal and the universal is what makes memoirs powerful—they're personal enough to evoke emotion, yet broad enough to connect with people from different backgrounds.

Memoirs also give the writer a chance to reflect on their past and understand how their experiences have shaped them. Writing a memoir can be a way to process emotions and find meaning in life events. By sharing these intimate stories, writers open up to their readers, creating a bond through shared struggles and victories. In the end, memoirs remind us that despite our differences, we all go through challenges and growth in our own ways.

One well-known example of a memoir is *Becoming* by Michelle Obama. In this book, she shares her personal journey from growing up on the South Side of Chicago to becoming the First Lady of the United States. The memoir explores her experiences with family, education, career, and public life, while also reflecting on the challenges she faced and the lessons she learned along the way. Through her story, Michelle Obama offers readers an intimate look at her personal struggles and triumphs, inspiring many with her resilience and honesty.

Personal Essays:

Personal essays give writers the chance to explore a topic from their own unique viewpoint, combining personal reflection with deeper analysis. Unlike formal essays, which focus on presenting facts or arguments, personal essays blend the writer's thoughts, emotions, and experiences with a broader understanding of the subject. This makes them more intimate and relatable to readers, allowing for a deeper connection.

In *The Opposite of Loneliness*, Marina Keegan's collection of essays beautifully demonstrates how personal experiences can be linked to universal themes. Keegan writes about her feelings of uncertainty and hope as she faced the transition from college to adulthood. These deeply personal reflections resonate with readers because they touch on themes that many people experience—such as finding one's place in the world and dealing with change. Her essays are engaging because they are authentic, making readers feel as though they are sharing her thoughts and emotions.

A good personal essay combines introspection with larger ideas, often prompting the reader to reflect on their own life. Joan Didion's essay *Goodbye to All That* uses her experience of living in New York to explore broader themes of belonging, change, and the passage of time. It's personal, yet relatable to anyone who has experienced a significant life shift. Personal essays allow writers to connect personal moments with universal truths, making them powerful tools for self-expression and engagement. By sharing their own stories, writers invite readers to reflect, relate, and perhaps see their own lives in a new light.

7.3. Blending Facts with Storytelling

The art of writing non-fiction often rests on the balance between factual accuracy and engaging storytelling. While the foundation of non-fiction lies in delivering truthful information, the challenge is to present these facts in a way that captivates and holds the reader's

> "The challenge of Nonfiction is to marry art and truth."
>
> _Phyllis Rose

attention. This is where storytelling comes into play. By weaving facts into a narrative that is both informative and compelling, writers can transform dry information into something that resonates emotionally and intellectually with readers.

Using Literary Devices

Incorporating literary devices such as metaphors, imagery, and dialogue can greatly enhance the storytelling aspect of non-fiction writing. These tools, typically associated with fiction, can bring life and colour to factual content. A great example of this is found in Luis Alberto Urrea's *The Devil's Highway*, which tells the true story of a group of Mexican immigrants who faced deadly conditions while trying to cross the U.S. border. Urrea uses vivid descriptions and narrative techniques that draw readers in, making the harsh realities of immigration feel immediate and personal. Through the use of literary elements, the facts become more than just data—they evoke emotion and create a lasting impact.

Structuring Information

How information is structured also plays a key role in keeping readers engaged. A well-organized non-fiction piece doesn't just present facts; it guides the reader through them in a way that's logical yet creative. One effective method is to structure the narrative around clear themes and subheadings, helping readers navigate through the material while maintaining their interest. Including anecdotes and real-life examples can further enhance this approach by making abstract or complex information more relatable. Stephen King, in his memoir *On Writing*, emphasizes the importance of storytelling in non-fiction, stating, *"The story is the thing, and the facts are what you use to flesh it out."* This highlights that while facts are essential, it's the story woven around them that truly engages the reader. The most effective non-fiction doesn't just inform—it tells a story. By blending factual accuracy with the tools of narrative, non-fiction writers can craft works that are both informative and deeply compelling.

7.4 Maintaining Authenticity and Accuracy

In non-fiction writing, creativity and storytelling are vital, but they must be balanced with a commitment to truth and authenticity. The integrity of a non-fiction work is rooted in its accuracy, and writers carry the responsibility of ensuring that the facts they present are reliable. While engaging readers through narrative is essential, the foundation of non-fiction lies in its truthful portrayal of real events, people, and ideas. Upholding this authenticity not only builds trust with the reader but also respects the complexity of the subjects being explored.

Fact-Checking and Verification

One of the core aspects of maintaining accuracy in non-fiction is rigorous fact-checking. Ensuring that every piece of information is verified through reliable sources is crucial to the credibility of the work. Non-fiction writers must consult multiple references and, when needed, seek the expertise of professionals in the relevant field. This thorough approach helps avoid mistakes that can undermine the trust between the writer and the audience.

Writing Prompt for essay

1. Think of an important moment in your life that changed your perspective. Write down the event, how it altered your views, and what you learned from the experience.
2. Remember a particular book or article that has influenced your understanding of a social issue. Note down the key arguments and how they impacted your views or actions.
3. Reflect on a personal goal you set and the journey you undertook to achieve it. Put together all the obstacles, the milestones you

Writing Prompt for Journaling

1. Write about a place you've visited that left a lasting impression on you. Pay attention to the sights, sounds, feelings you experienced, and write why you liked this place.
2. Think of a recent challenge you faced and write down details about it focusing on the strategies you used to overcome it and your experience with it.
3. Explore the impact of technology on your daily life. Write about how it has changed your routines, relationships, and overall well-being, and consider both positive and negative aspects.

In her book *The Journalist and the Murderer*, Janet Malcolm examines the ethical dilemmas faced by non-fiction writers, particularly in journalism. She stresses how errors or intentional manipulation of facts can have significant consequences, not only for the reputation of the writer but also for the subjects involved. Factual accuracy is more than a technical requirement—it's a moral responsibility. Readers trust non-fiction to provide an honest account, and when that trust is broken, it can have a lasting impact on the credibility of the writer and the work.

Maintaining authenticity and accuracy in non-fiction requires a combination of thorough research, ethical consideration, and respect for the truth. It's a process of weaving factual integrity into the narrative, ensuring that the story not only captivates but also upholds the trust and responsibility inherent in non-fiction writing. It is a careful balance of factual integrity and storytelling.

References

Capote, Truman. *In Cold Blood*. Vintage, 1994.

Didion, Joan. "Goodbye to All That." *Slouching Towards Bethlehem*, Farrar, Straus and Giroux, 1968.

Kalanithi, Paul. *When Breath Becomes Air*. Random House, 2016.

Karr, Mary. *The Art of Memoir*. HarperCollins, 2015, p. 6.

Karr, Mary. *The Liars' Club*. Viking, 1995.

Keegan, Marina. *The Opposite of Loneliness*. Edited by Anne Fadiman, Simon & Schuster, 2014.

Larson, Erik. *The Devil in the White City*. Crown, 2003.

Malcolm, Janet. *The Journalist and the Murderer*. Vintage, 1990.

McPhee, John. *Draft No. 4: On the Writing Process*. Farrar, Straus and Giroux, 2017, p. 157.

Obama, Michelle. *Becoming*. Crown, 2018.

Urrea, Luis Alberto. *The Devil's Highway: A True Story*. Little, Brown, 2004.

Westover, Tara. *Educated: A Memoir*. Random House, 2018.

Chapter 8

Scriptwriting

Scriptwriting is the architectural blueprint of performance, a specialized form of storytelling that translates words into visceral experiences for audiences. Unlike prose, which lives in the reader's imagination, scripts exist to be realized through collaboration—whether on stage, screen, or radio. This chapter explores how scriptwriters shape stories across three distinct mediums, each with its own language and limitations. It includes writing for the stage, crafting dialogue and scenes, the intricacies of screenwriting, the unique demands of writing for radio, and the elements that make a strong play or screenplay.

> "It's possible to make a bad movie out of a good script, but I can't make a good movie from a bad script."
>
> _ George Clooney

8.1. Writing for the Stage

Writing for the stage requires an acute understanding of dialogue and scene construction. In stage plays, dialogue is the primary tool for conveying character, advancing the plot, and creating tension. The constraints of space and movement on stage mean that every line must serve a purpose. In *Three Uses of the Knife*, David Mamet emphasizes that drama is inherently structured around conflict. He asserts that the essence of drama lies in the struggle and confrontation between opposing forces, and that this conflict is what engages the audience.

Crafting Effective Dialogue

Stage plays live and die by their dialogue. With no camera close-ups or editing to manipulate perspective, every word must pull triple duty: revealing character, advancing plot, and heightening conflict. The playwright's challenge lies in crafting exchanges where subtext simmers beneath the surface—what characters avoid saying often carries more weight than their actual words.

Building Scenes

Scenes in a play must be structured with rising tension, revealing crucial information about the characters and their relationships. Playwrights like Harold Pinter are known for using pauses and silences to heighten tension within a scene, as seen in *The Homecoming*, where the unspoken emotions between family members are as powerful as the dialogue. Crafting a strong scene involves balancing action with reaction, allowing characters to develop through their interactions. A great stage scene functions like a pressure cooker, with tension escalating through carefully orchestrated entrances, exits, and spatial relationships.

A Family Gathering

Write a scene set during a family dinner where long-held secrets are revealed, affecting the relationships of the family members. Focus on the dialogue and character interactions to build tension.

The Unexpected Guest

Create a short play where an unexpected guest arrives at a community meeting, bringing with them news or a challenge that forces the characters to confront their assumptions and prejudices.

8.2. Screenwriting

Screenwriting, while rooted in the same storytelling principles as stage plays, demands a more visual approach. Screenplays serve as blueprints for films and television, guiding directors, actors, and production teams in bringing a story to life. The format, structure, and focus on visual storytelling distinguish screenwriting from other forms of writing.

Formatting and Structure

Proper formatting is essential in screenwriting. Screenplays adhere to a specific format, where dialogue, scene descriptions, and action lines are laid out in a precise manner. Syd Field, in *Screenplay: The Foundations of Screenwriting*, emphasizes the importance of mastering this format, stating, *"A screenplay is a story told with pictures, in dialogue and description, and placed within the context of dramatic structure. It is the art of visual storytelling"* (Field 6) The industry-standard format allows screenplays to be easily read and interpreted by all members of a production team.

Structurally, most screenplays follow a three-act format: setup, confrontation, and resolution. In *The Hero's Journey* by Christopher Vogler, this structure is outlined in terms of the protagonist's journey, with key moments like the inciting incident, midpoint, and climax marking major turning points. For example, in *The Dark Knight*, the three-act structure is clear: Act One introduces Gotham's descent into chaos, Act Two escalates with the Joker's reign of terror, and Act Three resolves with Batman's ultimate sacrifice.

> "The difference between life and the movies is that a script has to make sense, and life doesn't."
>
> _Joseph L. Mankiewicz

Visual Storytelling

In screenwriting, visual storytelling is paramount. Screenwriters must think cinematically, crafting scenes that can be conveyed through images, sound, and action. As director and screenwriter Alfred Hitchcock once said, *"Dialogue should simply be a sound among other sounds."* (Hitchcock qtd, in Truffaut 48) In *Birdman*, written by Alejandro G. Iñárritu, the fluid, long takes and visual metaphors carry much of the film's narrative weight, illustrating how visuals can tell the story in a more dynamic way than dialogue alone.

8.3. Writing for Radio

Writing for radio comes with its own set of challenges because the story has to be told entirely through sound. Unlike other mediums, where visuals help convey meaning, radio scripts rely on dialogue, sound effects, and music to engage the audience and build the narrative. The listener's experience is shaped solely by what they hear, so every sound needs to count.

Creating Atmosphere through Sound

In radio, sound is everything. Writers need to think about how different noises will help set the scene and draw listeners into the story. For example, in the BBC's long-running radio drama *The Archers*, sound effects like birds chirping, footsteps, and doors opening are used to create the feeling of rural England. These subtle details help paint a picture in the listener's mind, even though there are no visuals. Sound effects are used to show action, such as a car driving away or a knock at the door, allowing the audience to follow the story without needing to see it. By carefully choosing and layering sounds, radio writers can build a vivid world that exists entirely in the listener's imagination.

> "The power of radio is not that it speaks to millions, but that it speaks intimately and privately to each one of those millions."
>
> _Hallie Flanagan

Dialogue and Character

Since there are no visual cues in radio, dialogue is the primary way to reveal character and move the story forward. The voices of the characters, along with the way they speak, must communicate everything about them—what they feel, who they are, and what's happening around them.

Daily News Roundup

Write a radio segment summarising the major news events of the day

Include interviews with experts or ordinary people affected by these events

It adds depth and variety to the broadcast

Local Hero Spotlight

Create a radio feature about a local individual who has made a significant impact on their community.

Use interviews, sound bites from community events

Use narrative storytelling to highlight their achievements and personal journey

Special Day Reflection

Write a a radio script for a special day, such as International Women's Day or Earth Day

Highlight various perspectives on the significance of the day

You can use interviews, historical context, and listener interactions

In Dylan Thomas's famous radio play *Under Milk Wood*, the distinct voices and poetic rhythm of the dialogue bring the fictional Welsh village of Llareggub to life. Every word matters in radio writing, as it must express emotion, build atmosphere, and reflect the personalities of the characters. Without facial expressions or body language, vocal tone and dialogue become the key tools to convey mood and tell the story. By focusing on sound, radio writers can create rich, immersive stories that captivate listeners through dialogue and the careful use of sound effects. In this way, they turn the limitations of the medium into its strengths, crafting narratives that live purely in the mind's ear.

Writing for the stage, screen, or radio requires a careful balance of creativity, technical skill, and collaboration. Whether you're crafting a play, screenplay, or radio script, the key elements of storytelling remain the same: strong conflict, well-developed characters, purposeful dialogue, and a clear structure. By mastering these elements, writers can create scripts that captivate audiences and stand the test of time. Whether you're writing an original work or adapting an existing story, the goal is always to tell a compelling, engaging story that resonates with viewers or listeners.

References

Field, Syd. *Screenplay: The Foundations of Screenwriting*. Expanded ed., Delta, 2005. p.6

Hitchcock, Alfred, and François Truffaut. *Hitchcock: The Definitive Study of Alfred Hitchcock by François Truffaut*. Revised ed., translated by Helen G. Scott, Simon & Schuster, 1984, p. 48.

Ibsen, Henrik. *A Doll's House*. Translated by Michael Meyer, Methuen, 1981.

Mamet, David. *Three Uses of the Knife: On the Nature and Purpose of Drama*. Vintage, 2000.

Nolan, Christopher, director. *The Dark Knight*. Performances by Christian Bale, Heath Ledger, and Aaron Eckhart, Warner Bros. Pictures, 2008.

Pinter, Harold. *The Homecoming*. Methuen Drama, 2007.

Thomas, Dylan. *Under Milk Wood: A Play for Voices*. New Directions, 1954.

Vogler, Christopher. *The Writer's Journey: Mythic Structure for Writers*. 3rd ed., Michael Wiese Productions, 2007.

Chapter 9

New Forms of Writing

In the constantly evolving landscape of creative writing, new forms have emerged, transforming the ways in which writers express themselves and connect with readers. From the rapid rise of digital platforms to the blending of visual art and text, these new forms push the boundaries of storytelling and offer fresh ways to communicate ideas, emotions, and experiences. This chapter explores a diverse range of new writing forms—from the bite-sized narratives of flash fiction to the expansive worlds of graphic novels, travel fiction, fanfiction, and more. Each form presents unique possibilities and challenges, allowing writers to experiment with structure, medium, and voice.

9.1. The Rise of Blogs

Blogs, once envisioned as simple online diaries, have evolved into a dynamic platform for creative expression. Today, bloggers from around the world use this medium not just to share personal reflections, but to comment on current events, explore specific interests, and engage with readers through creative nonfiction. Unlike traditional forms of writing, blogs offer a great deal of flexibility, allowing writers to decide how informal or structured they want their content to be. Whether it's a carefully curated essay or a casual update on daily life, a blog can adapt to the writer's style and objectives.

One of the most notable examples of modern blogging is Brandon Stanton's *Humans of New York*, which has significantly reshaped the way stories are told online. Through his blog, Stanton combines photography and personal interviews to capture snapshots of people's lives. These posts, though often brief, offer deep insight into the human experience. Stanton's blog bridges journalism, memoir, and storytelling, showcasing how blogs can transcend their original format and evolve into powerful tools for digital storytelling. This is an ability to mix genres highlights the versatility of blogs, which can range from personal reflections to more structured narratives, blending text with visuals to create compelling content.

One of the unique strengths of blogging is its immediacy. Unlike other forms of writing that may take months to reach an audience, blogs allow writers to publish instantly and engage directly with readers in real time. This immediacy fosters interaction, as bloggers can receive and respond to comments, adjust their content based on feedback, and even build a community around shared interests. The interactive nature of blogging sets it apart from traditional writing, creating a dialogue between the writer and their audience, often leading to a loyal readership and a more intimate connection with followers.

The range of topics that can be covered on blogs is virtually limitless. From travel and lifestyle to more complex themes like social justice and political commentary, blogs serve as a platform for writers to explore their passions and share them with the world. This diversity in content makes blogs a rich source of information and inspiration for readers. For writers, the freedom to explore various topics, experiment with style, and interact with their audience makes blogging an empowering and creative outlet.

In today's digital age, blogs have become a powerful tool for storytelling, allowing individuals to voice their thoughts, reflect on their experiences, and engage in larger public conversations. They blur the lines between personal writing and public discourse, making them an essential part of modern communication. Whether used to tell personal stories, comment on societal issues, or explore niche interests, blogs continue to redefine how we share and consume content online. Their flexibility and adaptability ensure that they remain a relevant and powerful medium for writers of all kinds.

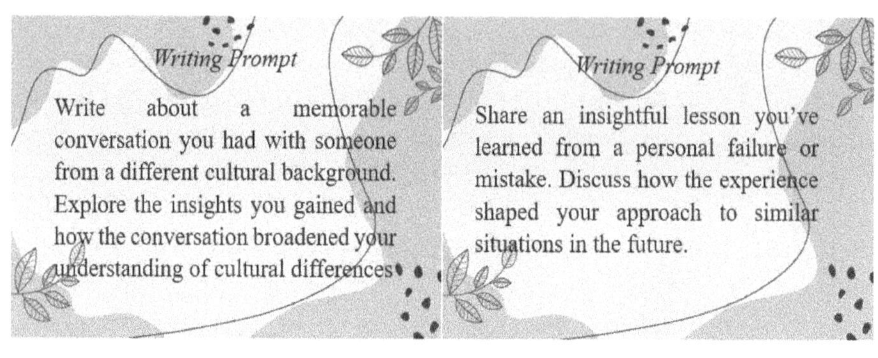

9.2. Flash Fiction

Flash fiction, often called "short-short stories" or "microfiction," is a unique form of storytelling that focuses on brevity without losing emotional depth or impact. With word counts typically ranging from 300 to 1,000 words, flash fiction requires writers to be precise and concise. The challenge is to create a full story in just a few words, which means every sentence and word must serve a clear purpose. This economy of language forces writers to focus on the most important aspects of the narrative, creating a powerful and often impactful experience for readers.

Writing Prompt

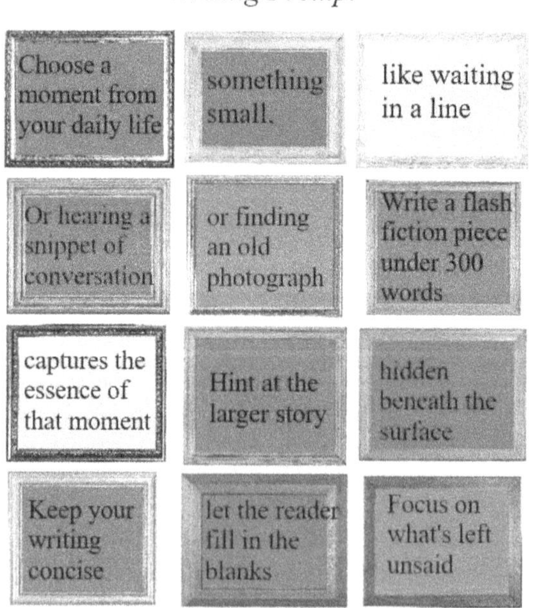

Today we live in a world where people are accustomed to consuming information quickly and efficiently, flash fiction has found a growing audience. Its brevity makes it perfect for readers who want a complete story but don't have the time or attention for longer works. Writers can deliver a lot in just a few paragraphs, packing emotion, conflict, and resolution into a small space. This makes flash fiction not only accessible but also ideal for modern platforms like blogs, social media, and online literary magazines, where short-form content thrives.

One of the most famous examples of flash fiction is Ernest Hemingway's six-word story: "For sale: baby shoes, never worn." Despite being incredibly short, this story evokes strong emotions and leaves much to the reader's imagination. This example demonstrates how much can be conveyed in just a few words. Although extreme in its brevity, Hemingway's story shows the potential of flash fiction to suggest complex backstories and emotions with minimal language.

Flash fiction thrives on implication. Writers don't spell out every detail; instead, they hint at what's happening, encouraging readers to fill in the blanks with their own imagination. This interaction between writer and reader creates a rich reading experience, where much of the story exists beyond what's written on the page. The ability to suggest so much with so little is what makes flash fiction such a powerful and engaging form of storytelling.

The art of flash fiction is crafting stories that linger in the reader's mind long after the last word is read. The stories manage to explore complex themes and emotions while leaving much unsaid. This style of writing challenges readers to look deeper, finding meaning in the spaces between the words. Flash fiction is a testament to the idea that sometimes less is more.

One of the main appeals of flash fiction is the challenge it presents to writers. To succeed in flash fiction, a writer must be skilled in stripping away unnecessary details and focusing on the heart of the story. Every word must earn its place. There's no room for rambling descriptions or long-winded explanations. The writer must capture the essence of the story quickly, while still making an emotional connection with the reader.

Despite its short length, flash fiction can cover a wide range of themes and genres. Whether it's a quick glimpse into a character's life, a surprising twist, or a moment of realization, flash fiction offers endless possibilities for creativity. Because it is so short, writers often use it to experiment with ideas or styles they might not try in longer works. The limitations of word count push writers to think outside the box and be inventive with how they tell their stories.

9.3. Graphic Novels: The Fusion of Art and Story

Graphic novels are a unique blend of visual art and storytelling that offer a powerful way to communicate narratives. While the format has roots in the comic book world, graphic novels have evolved into a respected literary genre. Today, they tackle complex themes, convey deep emotions, and tell stories that resonate on multiple levels. Examples like *Maus* by Art Spiegelman and *Persepolis* by Marjane Satrapi demonstrate how this form goes beyond simple entertainment, delving into historical, political, and personal experiences.

Maus is a prime example of the graphic novel's ability to handle heavy, real-world topics. In this work, Spiegelman tells the story of the Holocaust by using anthropomorphized characters—Jews are depicted as mice and Nazis as cats. This visual metaphor enhances the emotional weight of the narrative, making a tragic historical event feel more immediate and personal. Spiegelman's choice to combine text and imagery enables readers to experience the horror, loss, and survival in a way that traditional prose might struggle to achieve.

Similarly, *Persepolis* by Marjane Satrapi uses the graphic novel format to share her experiences growing up in revolutionary Iran. Satrapi's black-and-white illustrations capture the stark contrast between her childhood innocence and the harsh political realities around her. The combination of visual storytelling and Satrapi's personal reflections makes the political struggles of that era accessible and relatable to readers who may not be familiar with the history of Iran. By using images, Satrapi adds emotional layers that bring her story to life in a way that mere words could not.

One of the most compelling aspects of graphic novels is their ability to deliver multi-layered storytelling. With images and text working together, the reader experiences both visual and written storytelling at the same time, which creates a rich and immersive narrative. Unlike traditional novels, which rely heavily on descriptive language to set the scene and develop characters, graphic novels allow writers to "show" rather than "tell." Visuals convey mood, setting, and even subtle character emotions, while the text—often in the form of dialogue or internal thoughts—moves the plot forward. This combination creates a dynamic rhythm that guides readers through the story, blending the fast pace of visual cues with the thoughtful progression of words.

Graphic novels also have a unique capacity for non-linear storytelling. In *Watchmen* by Alan Moore, for instance, the story is told through a complex interweaving of different timelines and perspectives. The use of visual motifs, colour schemes, and panel arrangements helps the reader navigate the shifting narratives, building layers of meaning that would be difficult to achieve in a traditional novel. Moore uses these visual techniques to explore deep themes of morality, power, and human nature, challenging readers to think critically about the story while being immersed in its world.

The versatility of graphic novels makes them a perfect medium for experimentation. Writers and illustrators can collaborate to push the boundaries of how stories are told, using both text and image to engage the reader in fresh, innovative ways. In a graphic novel, the visuals don't just support the story; they are an integral part of it. This creates opportunities for writers to explore new forms of storytelling, from non-linear narratives to abstract themes, in ways that engage the imagination of readers more fully.

9.4. Travel Fiction

Travel fiction is a genre that brings together the excitement of discovering new places with the art of storytelling. Through fictional characters and plots, it offers readers the chance to experience different parts of the world in a unique and imaginative way. While traditional travel writing is often based on personal experiences, travel fiction allows for the blending of real places with fictional events, adding emotional and transformative layers to the narrative.

One well-known example of this genre is Elizabeth Gilbert's *Eat, Pray, Love*. In this memoir-turned-fictional journey, Gilbert takes readers on an exploration of Italy, India, and Indonesia. Although the book is rooted in the author's real-life experiences, it adopts many elements of travel fiction, especially in the way it delves into the emotional and spiritual growth that accompanies physical travel. The locations in *Eat, Pray, Love* serve as more than just places; they represent stages in the protagonist's personal journey toward self-discovery and healing. Each destination reflects an internal struggle or transformation, turning the book into a layered narrative about both the physical and emotional aspects of travel.

Travel fiction thrives on the contrast between the known and the unknown. It taps into the universal desire to explore new places and push the boundaries of what's familiar. Whether it's an outer journey to a distant location or an inner journey of self-discovery, this genre reflects the transformative power of travel. In *The Beach* by Alex Garland, the protagonist's journey to a hidden island in Thailand leads to a deeper exploration of idealism, community, and the darker side of human nature. The island itself, while real, becomes a symbol for the protagonist's internal struggles, blending the beauty and mystery of the location with the complexities of the human experience.

Travel fiction allows writers to infuse real places with fictional narratives that highlight both the geography and the essence of a location. The streets, landscapes, and local cultures become integral to the story, shaping the characters' experiences. The genre invites readers to see places not only as settings but as dynamic, living elements that impact the characters' emotional journeys. For instance, in *Shantaram* by Gregory David Roberts, the vibrant streets of Mumbai are more than just a backdrop; they shape the protagonist's entire identity and journey of survival and redemption.

Travel fiction offers more than just an exploration of new locations. It allows readers to connect with the deeper emotional and psychological impact of travel, turning every destination into a character in its own right. Through characters' adventures, conflicts, and discoveries, travel fiction opens a window to the world, reminding us of the power of place to shape who we are and how we grow.

9.5. Fanfiction:

Fanfiction, once relegated to niche online communities, has emerged as a significant cultural phenomenon, reshaping the way readers and writers interact with popular works of fiction. Fanfiction allows writers to take established characters and worlds from books, films, and TV shows and reimagine them in new contexts, scenarios, or relationships. Whether it's filling in the gaps of Harry Potter or exploring alternate universes in Star Wars, fanfiction serves as a form of participatory storytelling that builds on the work of others. What makes fanfiction unique is its collaborative nature. Writers engage with readers, often receiving immediate feedback and adjusting their stories accordingly. The fanfiction community thrives on shared enthusiasm for the source material, creating a space where creativity and fandom intersect. Sites like Wattpad and Archive of Our Own (AO3) have become major platforms where fanfiction writers share their work, attracting millions of readers and reshaping the boundaries between fandom and literature. Fanfiction is also a space for subverting traditional narratives. Many fanfiction writers use the genre to explore marginalized perspectives, reimagine romantic pairings, or push back against established plotlines.

In doing so, fanfiction becomes a form of creative freedom that democratizes storytelling, allowing anyone with passion and imagination to contribute to the cultural conversation.

9.6. Podcasts and Audio Stories

In today's digital age, podcasts and audio stories are breathing new life into the ancient art of oral storytelling. Long before written texts became the dominant medium, stories were shared through spoken word, passed down from generation to generation. Now, with the rise of podcast platforms such as *Serial*, *Welcome to Night Vale*, and *The Moth*, this tradition is being revived in exciting and creative ways. Podcasts and audio stories encompass a wide range of genres, from true crime and memoirs to fictional worlds, showcasing how versatile and powerful sound-based storytelling can be. Writing for audio presents its own set of challenges. Since there are no visual aids, the narrative must rely entirely on sound—voice, music, and sound effects. The language used in audio stories needs to be vivid and descriptive to help listeners picture the scene in their minds. Rhythm and pacing also play an important role in creating an engaging listening experience. Dialogue becomes a key tool for conveying character and emotion, and the narrator's voice serves as the emotional core of the story, connecting directly with the audience. Audio stories have a unique ability to create a personal, intimate experience for listeners. Whether they are scripted or improvised, these stories allow audiences to feel like they are part of the narrative. With nothing but a voice and some well-placed sound effects, audio stories can transport listeners into a world filled with emotion and atmosphere.

New Frontier of Creative Writing

Creative writing has expanded far beyond traditional forms, opening a world of opportunities for experimentation with new media, formats, and genres. From the short, punchy format of flash fiction to the visually immersive graphic novel, each form offers fresh ways to tell stories. The digital age brings platforms like blogs and podcasts, which allow for more interactive and participatory storytelling. As technology evolves, so does the art of writing, pushing the boundaries of creativity and opening up countless new avenues for writers to explore.

References

Garland, Alex. *The Beach*. Penguin, 2005.

Gilbert, Elizabeth. *Eat, Pray, Love* . Riverhead Books, 2017.

Gregory David Roberts. *Shantaram*. St. Martin's Press, 2004.

Moore, Alan, and Dave Gibbons. *Watchmen*. Dc Comics, 2019.

Spiegelman, Art. *The Complete Maus*. 1996. Penguin, 2003.

Stanton, Brandon. "Humans of New York." *Humans of New York*, 2019, www.humansofnewyork.com/.

"The Moth | Podcast." *The Moth*, themoth.org/podcast.

"Welcome to Night Vale." *WELCOME to NIGHT VALE*, www.welcometonightvale.com/.

Part III:

Taking Your Writing to the Next Level

Chapter 10

Finding Your Style of Writing

Finding your writing style is not a process that unfolds instantly; it's a gradual evolution, often shaped by experimentation, self-reflection, and external influences. How do you create something distinct in a landscape filled with countless voices from the past and present? The development of a unique writing voice is an ongoing journey. For many writers, this process feels elusive, particularly when faced with the challenge of originality.

10.1. The Myth of Originality: Learning from Other Writers

One of the key truths about writing, though difficult to accept, is that all writers borrow from others. This reality poses an interesting paradox: while the goal may be to create something original, the foundation of any writer's voice is built upon the work of others. T.S. Eliot's famous line, *"Immature poets imitate; mature poets steal; bad poets deface what they take, and good poets make it into something better, or at least something different."* (Eliot 59) captures this dynamic well. Every writer, whether consciously or not, draws from the styles, structures, and themes of those who have come before. However, originality arises not from avoiding influence, but from transforming these influences into something that feels unique and personal.

Writing style often develops through this interaction of external inspiration and personal perspective. Whether you are influenced by the succinct style of Ernest Hemingway, the lyrical prose of Virginia Woolf, or the sharp wit of George Orwell, or any contemporary writer you love, your writing will inevitably reflect what you've read. Reading widely allows you to explore a variety of voices, gradually helping you identify what resonates with your own sensibilities.

The journey from imitation to originality is a natural progression for writers. Raymond Carver, an acclaimed short story writer, began his career heavily influenced by Hemingway's concise style. Over time, Carver's voice developed its own distinctive character, marked by emotional depth and minimalism that became quintessentially "Carveresque." Rather than fearing the influence of other writers, embracing it can become the gateway to discovering your own unique voice.

10.2. The Elements of Writing Style

To find your writing style, it is essential to understand the various components that shape a writer's voice. Writing style is not just about the choice of words; it encompasses multiple aspects, such as language, rhythm, and subject matter, that work together to define how you express yourself on the page.

Word Choice and Language

The words you select play a significant role in defining your style. Some writers lean toward simple, direct language, much like Hemingway, while others opt for intricate, metaphor-rich prose, similar to Toni Morrison. Word choice reflects more than just preference—it aligns with the tone, mood, and emotional impact you want to achieve. William Zinsser, in *On Writing Well*, emphasizes that good writers use language efficiently by keeping it clear and precise.

However, effective writing doesn't necessarily mean using simple language. Consider Salman Rushdie, whose novel *Midnight's Children* is full of lush, descriptive passages that complement the complexity of the narrative. Your voice will naturally emerge as you experiment with language that matches the themes, characters, and emotions in your stories.

Sentence Structure and Rhythm

The way you structure your sentences also shapes your writing style. Some writers, like Cormac McCarthy, are known for their long, flowing sentences, often with sparse punctuation, creating a distinctive rhythm that defines their voice. Others, like Margaret Atwood in *The*

Handmaid's Tale, use shorter, fragmented sentences to convey tension and urgency.

Experimenting with sentence structures—whether they are brief and crisp or elaborate and winding—allows you to find the rhythm that fits your narrative. Reading your work aloud is a helpful way to understand how the flow of your sentences shapes the reader's experience.

Themes and Subject Matter

Another important aspect of style is the themes you return to in your writing. Writers, much like visual artists, often explore recurring motifs across their work. For instance, Haruki Murakami frequently delves into themes of loneliness, surrealism, and the tension between reality and dreams. His voice is defined not just by his writing technique, but by the thematic material that characterizes his stories.

Identifying the themes that resonate with you—whether they revolve around identity, power dynamics, or existential questions—will help refine your voice. By consistently addressing certain topics, you will develop a signature style that reflects your core interests and emotional truths.

10.3. External Influences

Beyond the conscious decisions of language, rhythm, and themes, several external factors influence your writing voice. These influences, often beyond your control, shape your worldview and thus affect the way you express yourself in writing.

Reading and Influence

As discussed, reading widely is one of the most powerful tools for discovering your voice. Every writer learns techniques and styles from others. You may appreciate the way Alice Munro develops character subtly or how Zadie Smith weaves dialogue with internal monologue. As you read, your voice is enriched by absorbing not only styles but also the way other writers navigate themes, structure stories, and approach language.

Reading with intention is key to this process. When reading, take note of what works and why. Ask yourself how Jhumpa Lahiri creates intimacy between her characters or how Kazuo Ishiguro evokes such deep emotional resonance through understated prose. These lessons will seep into your own writing, but over time, they will evolve into something distinctly yours.

Cultural and Social Context

Your background, culture, and the social environment you inhabit also contribute significantly to shaping your voice. Writers like Chimamanda Ngozi Adichie and Junot Díaz weave their cultural identities into their narratives, making their stories feel both universal and deeply personal. Your writing voice will naturally carry the imprint of your experiences and the lens through which you view the world.

Consider how your cultural heritage, social environment, and personal experiences shape your perspective as a writer. These aspects are not only valuable influences but also unique to you. Embracing them allows your voice to become more authentic and representative of who you are.

10.4. Internal Influences: Writing from Within

While external influences play an important role, your writing voice is also shaped by internal factors—your emotions, beliefs, and the way you relate to your work.

Emotional Honesty

A strong writing voice often emerges when you write with emotional authenticity. Readers connect deeply with writing that feels raw and truthful, even in fiction. Joan Didion, known for her essays and memoirs, writes with a voice that is both sharp and deeply introspective, reflecting her inner struggles and fears. This level of emotional honesty makes her work compelling and relatable.

Finding your voice requires you to tap into your emotional core and be vulnerable on the page. Whether writing fiction, non-fiction, or poetry, allowing your authentic emotions to shine through will create a style that resonates with readers.

Personal Function of Literature

Understanding why you write is another internal influence on your voice. Writers who approach literature as a tool for intellectual exploration, like Milan Kundera, often have a more contemplative, philosophical style. Others, like J.K. Rowling, who writes with the goal of entertaining readers, may have a voice that leans toward imaginative and whimsical storytelling. Reflecting on your reasons for writing— whether it's to explore difficult truths, escape reality, or challenge norms—will shape the tone, themes, and style of your work.

10.5. Practical Steps to Finding Your Style

Now that we've explored the various components of writing style, let's look at some practical steps for discovering and refining your unique voice.

Free Writing: Free writing is one of the most effective ways to uncover your authentic voice. Setting aside time to write without any expectations, rules, or structure allows you to tap into your natural rhythms and patterns. Over time, you'll notice stylistic tendencies that emerge organically, whether it's a preference for descriptive prose or dialogue-heavy scenes.

Journaling: Journaling offers another avenue to explore your writing style. Since journals are private, there's less pressure to conform to specific writing standards, allowing your true voice to surface. Through journaling, you can track the stylistic patterns and themes that recur in your writing and apply them to more formal pieces.

Experimenting with Style

Another key step is to mimic the styles of writers you admire. This might seem counterintuitive, but by trying to emulate the tone of Virginia Woolf or the conciseness of Hemingway, you can better understand what fits your voice and what doesn't. As you experiment, your voice will emerge from the fusion of these influences and your unique perspective.

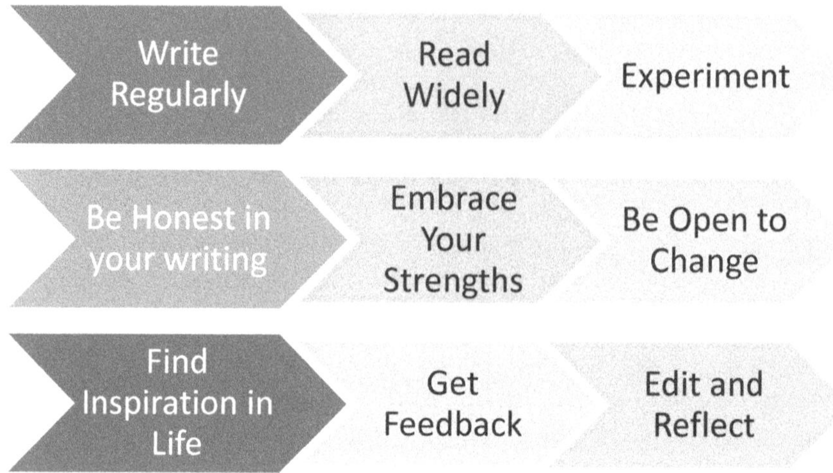

Read Widely and Diversely

Reading a variety of books is important for improving your writing skills and expanding your understanding of different styles, genres, and viewpoints. When you read widely, you gain insights and inspiration that can help shape your own work. Exploring different genres, such as classic literature, contemporary fiction, and non-fiction, exposes you to various storytelling techniques. For instance, authors like Toni Morrison, Haruki Murakami, and Chimamanda Ngozi Adichie each have unique styles that can enrich your perspective as a writer. In addition, reading literature from different cultures allows you to appreciate diverse experiences and viewpoints, which can help you create more realistic and relatable characters. For example, the works of Chinua Achebe and Jean Rhys offer valuable insights into African and Caribbean cultures. Furthermore, studying literary classics can teach you important writing techniques. Books by authors like Shakespeare, Charles Dickens, and Jane Austen provide timeless lessons in how to develop characters, structure plots, and explore themes effectively. By immersing yourself in various reading materials, you not only gain a wider perspective but also deepen your understanding of the craft of writing. This broader knowledge will ultimately influence and improve your own writing, making it richer and more engaging for readers. Embracing diverse literature will inspire you to experiment with your own style and help you find your unique voice as a writer.

Engage in Writing Workshops and Courses

Participating in writing workshops and courses is an excellent way to improve your writing skills and connect with fellow writers who share your passion for storytelling. These workshops provide valuable feedback from both peers and experienced mentors, helping you identify the strengths and weaknesses in your writing. Many online workshops offer opportunities for constructive criticism, allowing you to refine your work and gain new perspectives.

In addition, writing courses introduce you to various techniques and approaches that can enhance your writing style. Through structured lessons and creative exercises, you can learn different aspects of writing, such as character development, plot structure, and dialogue. Online workshops are particularly beneficial because they offer flexibility, allowing you to participate from the comfort of your home while accessing resources from around the world.

Workshops and courses create opportunities to network with other writers, fostering a supportive community where you can exchange feedback and ideas. Engaging with fellow writers can lead to collaborations, inspiration, and friendships that enrich your writing journey. Many writing communities also provide platforms for sharing your work and discussing different writing styles, which can further enhance your understanding of the craft.

Seeking Inspiration from Life Experiences

Finding inspiration from your own life experiences can make your writing more genuine and relatable. When you write about your personal experiences, feelings, and thoughts, you bring real emotion and depth to your work. Observing the world around you—like the people you meet, the places you visit, and the events you witness—can spark new ideas for your stories. Writers like Charles Dickens were known for their sharp observations of society, showing how everyday life can inspire interesting narratives. Another way to find inspiration is by exploring different perspectives. Engaging with diverse experiences through reading, traveling, and meeting people from various backgrounds can help you see things in new ways. This broader understanding can lead to fresh ideas and insights for your writing. By tapping into your own experiences and being mindful of the world around you, you can keep your writing engaging and relevant. This approach allows you to connect with your readers on a deeper level, making your stories more impactful.

10.6. Voice is an Evolution

Finding your writing style is an ongoing journey that shifts as you evolve personally and creatively. It's not fixed—your style grows with your experiences, emotions, and changing perspective. The more you read, explore new genres, experiment with forms, and learn from others, the closer you get to understanding your unique voice. Stay open, curious, and willing to reflect who you are in the moment. Emotional honesty is key. When your writing is sincere, it resonates deeply. Authenticity creates connection. Writing is a path of self-discovery, and your style should grow alongside you as you continue to reflect, learn, and create.

References

Eliot, T. S. *The Sacred Wood: Essays on Poetry and Criticism.* Methune, 1920, p. 59.

Zinsser, William. *On Writing Well: The Classic Guide to Writing Nonfiction.* Harperperennial, 2016.

Chapter 11

Revising and Editing Your Work

Revising and editing are essential steps in shaping your writing into its best form. These stages allow you to look at your draft with fresh eyes, refine its content, and ensure clarity and flow. The goal is not just to correct small mistakes but to take a deep look at the structure, language, and overall impact of your work. This process is what turns an initial draft into something polished and ready for others to read.

Rewriting and revising are more than just fixing grammar or spelling errors. These phases give you the chance to rethink your work, making sure it reflects your intended message and style. Often, when you finish a draft, you might not see its flaws right away because you're too close to the material. Revising helps you step back and view your manuscript from a reader's perspective. It's a chance to ask yourself questions like: Is the story clear? Are the characters well-developed? Does each part of the text contribute to the whole?

During revision, you might change large sections of your writing, add new elements, or cut parts that don't add value. Sometimes, this can mean completely reworking scenes, dialogue, or the structure of your story. It can be hard to make these changes, but they are necessary for creating a strong piece of writing.

11.1. Important Aspects of Revising and Editing

Focus on Content First

In the early stages of revision, focus on the big picture. This means concentrating on content rather than details like spelling or punctuation. Look at whether your writing achieves the purpose you set out with. Does the story flow naturally? Are the arguments in your essay strong and well-supported? Do the characters in your story have depth and believability? These are all important elements to review before focusing on minor details.

Editing for Clarity and Precision

Once you've addressed the broader issues through revision, it's time to move on to editing. Editing is about fine-tuning the details. This is where you ensure that your sentences are clear, concise, and free of errors. It's a more technical process that focuses on grammar, punctuation, word choice, and sentence structure.

Editing helps to make sure your writing is easy to understand and enjoyable to read. It's also a time to remove unnecessary words or phrases that may distract the reader. You want every sentence to serve a purpose. Reading your work out loud during the editing phase can be helpful. It allows you to hear how the words sound, making it easier to catch awkward phrases or unclear passages.

The Role of Feedback

Getting feedback from others is a critical part of revising and editing. When you've worked on a piece for a long time, it's easy to miss mistakes or overlook areas that might confuse the reader. Sharing your work with trusted readers or writers can give you fresh insights and suggestions for improvement.

The Revision Process

Revising your work is an important part of writing, and it involves much more than just fixing spelling or grammar mistakes. It's about taking a step back to look at the big picture and making sure that the structure, plot, and characters all come together to tell a clear and engaging story. At this stage, you might need to make significant changes that will improve the flow and depth of your manuscript. This process can feel challenging, but it's key to turning your draft into a polished and effective piece of writing.

Structural Revisions

One of the first things to address during the revision process is the structure of your manuscript. The structure is how your story is built—

it's what holds everything together. Ask yourself if the plot makes sense and if the events happen in a logical order. Does the story have a clear beginning, middle, and end? Are there any confusing parts that could make readers lose interest?

Sometimes, this means moving scenes around to make sure the story flows better. You might need to shorten or lengthen certain sections to improve pacing or even rewrite entire chapters to better serve the overall narrative. These kinds of changes may seem daunting, but they're necessary to ensure your story feels complete and easy to follow.

Character Development

Next, take a close look at your characters. Well-developed characters are what make a story come alive for readers. Think about how your characters change throughout the story. Are their actions and emotions believable? Do their motivations make sense? Readers need to connect with your characters, and for that to happen, your characters should feel real, with strengths, weaknesses, and goals that evolve as the plot unfolds.

If a character doesn't feel fully fleshed out, you might need to add more backstory or adjust their dialogue to better reflect who they are. Pay attention to consistency as well—characters should behave in ways that make sense based on their personalities and previous experiences. Inconsistencies can pull readers out of the story and make it harder for them to stay invested in the outcome.

Plot and Pacing

After addressing structure and characters, focus on the plot and pacing. A good story keeps readers hooked from beginning to end. Review the plot to make sure the events unfold naturally and that each part of the story serves a purpose. Are there sections that feel too slow, or parts where the action is too rushed? Proper pacing builds tension, keeps the story exciting, and maintains the reader's interest throughout.

Sometimes, adding or cutting scenes can help improve pacing. If a section feels slow or unnecessary, it might be better to remove it. On the other hand, if certain parts of the story feel rushed, you might want to add more details or scenes to give readers time to fully absorb what's happening.

11.2. Tips for Self-Editing

11.3. Working with Feedback and Beta Readers

Receiving feedback is an essential part of improving your writing. It's difficult to catch every issue on your own, and outside perspectives can help you see your work in a new light. Beta readers and critique partners can identify areas that need improvement, provide suggestions, and highlight strengths you may not have noticed. Working with feedback requires an open mind and a willingness to make changes that strengthen your manuscript.

Selecting Beta Readers

Choosing the right beta readers is crucial for getting useful feedback. These should be people who understand your genre and the kind of story you're trying to tell. For example, if you're writing science fiction, your beta readers should be familiar with that genre so they can give informed feedback on how well your story fits into it. Readers who regularly enjoy the type of book you've written are more likely to catch genre-specific issues and can help you understand whether your story will resonate with your intended audience.

It's also important to choose beta readers who will give you honest, constructive criticism. While friends and family may be supportive, they may not always provide the detailed, critical feedback you need to improve your work. Look for beta readers who are comfortable giving honest input and who will point out both strengths and weaknesses in your manuscript.

Providing Clear Instructions

To get the most out of your beta readers, it's helpful to give them clear instructions. Tell them what specific areas you want feedback on. For example, you might ask them to focus on character development, pacing, or plot coherence. Providing a list of questions can guide them in giving feedback that's useful to you. Sample questions could include: Are the characters relatable? Does the story keep your interest? Are there any confusing parts? By guiding their focus, you help beta readers provide targeted feedback that addresses the areas you care about most.

Analysing Feedback

When you receive feedback, it's important to approach it with an open mind. Some feedback might not match your vision for the story, and that's okay. Not every suggestion will work for you, but it's important to look for patterns in the feedback. If multiple beta readers point out the same issue, it's likely worth considering a revision in that area.

Try not to take negative feedback personally. Remember that beta readers are trying to help you improve your manuscript, not criticize you as a writer. Keep your overall goals in mind, and use the feedback that aligns with your vision for the story to make improvements. At the same time, don't be afraid to dismiss feedback that doesn't fit your creative direction.

Revising Based on Feedback

Once you've gathered feedback, it's time to start revising. Focus on the suggestions that you think will make your story stronger. If several readers mentioned the same issue, like a confusing plot point or a character that feels underdeveloped, make those areas your priority. Use their insights to revise and polish your manuscript, while staying true to your original vision.

Feedback can help you spot weaknesses and build on strengths. Incorporating useful suggestions will enhance your manuscript and get it closer to being the best version of itself. Working with beta readers can be a rewarding process, giving you fresh perspectives that you might not have considered otherwise.

11.4. Before Final Submission

Once you've finished revising your manuscript and included any feedback you've received, it's time to get your work ready for submission. This final stage is all about making sure your writing is polished and meets professional standards. Here are the steps you should take:

Final Proofreading

Go through your manuscript one last time to catch any errors in spelling, grammar, or punctuation. This is an important step to ensure that your writing looks clean and professional. Even small mistakes can distract from your work, so it's essential to make sure everything is correct.

Formatting

Make sure your manuscript follows the formatting guidelines required by agents or publishers. These might include specific instructions about margins, font size, spacing, or page numbers. Following these guidelines not only shows that you pay attention to detail but also makes your manuscript easier to read and review.

Crafting a Strong Query Letter

If you plan to send your manuscript to agents or publishers, you'll need to write a query letter. This letter should briefly introduce your work, highlight its strengths, and explain why it's a good fit for the agent or publisher. A strong query letter helps make a positive first impression and increases the chances of your manuscript being considered.

Preparing Submission Materials

In addition to your manuscript, you may need to prepare other materials for submission, such as a synopsis (a summary of the story) or an author bio (information about you and your writing background). Make sure all of these documents are carefully written, clear, and professionally presented.

Conclusion:

Revising and editing are essential stages in crafting a compelling manuscript. They go far beyond correcting surface-level errors—they involve a deep, thoughtful reworking of your writing. During revision, you focus on the heart of your story, refining plot structures, developing characters, and ensuring that the pacing keeps readers engaged. It's a process that requires a critical eye, the ability to step back and see your work from a new perspective, and the courage to make substantial changes where necessary. Editing, on the other hand, fine-tunes the details. This is where you polish your language, tighten your sentences, and ensure that your grammar, spelling, and punctuation are flawless. Careful editing ensures that your manuscript is clear, professional, and enjoyable to read. Both stages—revision and editing—are equally important in turning your draft into a polished piece.

Chapter 12

Publishing Your Work

Publishing your work is an exciting and important step in sharing your writing with the world. It marks the transition from a personal project to something that can be enjoyed by a wider audience. The process, however, can be complex and filled with choices, so it's essential to understand the different options available.

One of the primary decisions you'll face is choosing between traditional publishing and self-publishing. Traditional publishing typically involves working with literary agents, submitting your manuscript to publishing houses, and having your book professionally edited, marketed, and distributed. This path offers credibility and a team to support your work, but it can be competitive, and authors often have less control over the final product.

Self-publishing, on the other hand, provides full creative control and the ability to manage every aspect of your book, from editing and design to pricing and distribution. With the rise of digital platforms like e-books and print-on-demand services, self-publishing has become more accessible than ever. It allows authors to publish on their own terms, but it requires more effort in areas such as marketing and reaching readers.

In addition to these two paths, there are opportunities in submitting your work to literary journals, contests, or online platforms that specialize in shorter pieces or niche genres. E-books and online platforms also offer authors an easy way to connect directly with their audience, expanding their reach globally. By understanding these various options, you can confidently choose the best route for your work. Whether aiming for traditional publishing or taking the self-publishing route, the goal remains the same: to share your voice and story with readers everywhere.

12.1. Understanding the Publishing Process

The publishing process is a multi-stage journey that begins when your manuscript is ready to move beyond your desk. This stage is essential for transitioning from a writer to a published author and involves several critical steps.

The Manuscript Journey: The journey of a manuscript starts with the decision of how you want to publish your work. The traditional publishing route typically involves submitting your manuscript to established publishers, who handle editing, design, production, and marketing. This path can offer significant exposure and professional support but often involves a lengthy approval process. Self-publishing, on the other hand, requires you to manage or outsource all aspects of the publishing process, providing greater control but also demanding more effort and investment. Hybrid publishing merges aspects of both, offering professional support while allowing you more control.

Traditional Publishing: Traditional publishing is often seen as the gold standard in the literary world. This process begins with finding a literary agent who believes in your work and can represent it to publishers. Once an agent is secured, they will submit your manuscript to publishers, negotiate terms, and handle various aspects of the publishing deal. Traditional publishers provide extensive services, including editing, cover design, and marketing. They also manage distribution, getting your book into bookstores and online platforms. However, the path to acceptance can be long and competitive, with publishers and agents receiving numerous submissions and only accepting a small percentage.

Self-Publishing:

Self-publishing has become increasingly popular due to the control and flexibility it offers authors. When self-publishing, you retain all rights to your work and are responsible for every aspect of the publishing process, from editing to cover design to marketing. Self-publishing platforms like Amazon Kindle Direct Publishing (KDP), Smashwords, and IngramSpark allow you to publish your book in both digital and print formats. While this route provides greater creative freedom and higher royalties, it also requires you to manage all promotional efforts, which can be time-consuming and costly. Authors must be prepared to handle the complexities of the publishing process, including formatting, cover design, and distribution.

Hybrid Publishing:

Hybrid publishing is a relatively new model that combines elements of both traditional and self-publishing. In this model, authors work with a publishing company that provides professional services—such as editing, design, and marketing—while allowing the author to retain some control over the process. Hybrid publishers often require an upfront fee or a shared investment in the book's success. This model can be appealing to authors who want the benefits of professional support without fully relinquishing control. However, it is crucial to research hybrid publishers carefully, as the quality and terms of their services can vary widely.

Submission Preparation:

Preparing your manuscript for submission involves several key steps. First, ensure your manuscript is polished and follows industry standards for formatting. This typically includes using a standard font (e.g., Times New Roman, 12-point), double-spacing, and including page numbers. Next, craft a compelling query letter that introduces your manuscript and yourself. A query letter should include a brief synopsis of your work, a description of your writing background, and any relevant credentials or previous publications. Additionally, prepare a concise synopsis of your manuscript, highlighting the main plot points and character arcs. Tailor your submission materials to each publisher's or agent's guidelines to increase your chances of success.

12.2. Traditional vs. Self-Publishing

Choosing between traditional and self-publishing is a significant decision that depends on various factors, including your goals, resources, and preferences. Each option has its own set of characteristics that can influence your decision.

Traditional Publishing:

Pros: Traditional publishing offers numerous advantages, including professional editing, design, and marketing services. Publishers have established networks for book distribution, including bookstores and online retailers, which can increase the visibility and reach of your work. Being published by a reputable publisher can also lend credibility to your book, potentially attracting more readers and media attention. Additionally, traditional publishers often provide advances against royalties, which can provide financial support during the writing process.

Cons: The traditional publishing process can be lengthy and competitive. Securing a literary agent and getting a publishing deal may take months or even years. Publishers may also have specific preferences and may not accept manuscripts that fall outside their current focus. Authors have less control over the final product, including cover design and marketing strategies. Furthermore, advances are often recouped from future royalties, which means you may not see additional income until your book earns back its advance.

Self-Publishing:

Pros: Self-publishing offers complete control over the content, design, and marketing of your book. You can set your own timeline and make decisions about every aspect of the publishing process. Self-publishing platforms typically allow for higher royalty rates compared to traditional publishing, meaning you could potentially earn more per book sold. This route also provides flexibility in publishing niche or unconventional works that may not fit traditional publishing criteria. Additionally, self-publishing allows for immediate publication once your book is ready, bypassing the lengthy approval process of traditional publishing.

Cons: Self-publishing requires a significant investment of time and money. Authors are responsible for all aspects of production, including editing, design, and marketing, which can be overwhelming. Building visibility and credibility without the backing of a traditional publisher can be challenging. Marketing and promoting a self-published book often require substantial effort and resources, and authors must be prepared to engage in various promotional activities to reach their target audience.

Hybrid Publishing:

Pros: Hybrid publishing offers a blend of traditional and self-publishing benefits. Authors receive professional services such as editing, design, and marketing while maintaining some control over the process. This model can be advantageous for authors who want support but also wish to retain creative control. Hybrid publishers often have established networks for distribution and marketing, which can enhance the visibility of your book. Additionally, hybrid publishing can provide a more predictable timeline for publication compared to traditional publishing.

Cons: Hybrid publishers often require upfront fees or shared investment, which can be a barrier for some authors. The quality and extent of services provided can vary widely among hybrid publishers, so thorough research is necessary. Authors may also face challenges in assessing the value of the services offered and ensuring that they align with their publishing goals. It is important to carefully review contracts and terms before committing to a hybrid publishing arrangement.

Choosing the Right Path: When deciding between traditional, self-publishing, and hybrid publishing, consider factors such as your target audience, budget, desired level of control, and long-term goals. Reflect on your strengths and preferences—whether you value professional support and wider distribution or prefer creative control and flexibility. Each path has its trade-offs, and the best choice will align with your individual needs and aspirations. Additionally, consider consulting with other authors who have taken similar paths to gain insights and advice based on their experiences.

12.3. The World of E-Books and Online Platforms

The rise of digital technology has transformed the publishing landscape, offering new opportunities and challenges for authors. E-books and online platforms have become integral to modern publishing, providing innovative ways to reach readers.

E-Books:

E-books offer numerous benefits, including cost-effectiveness and convenience. They are accessible to readers worldwide, allowing you to reach a global audience without the need for physical distribution. E-books can be instantly downloaded and read on various devices, such as e-readers, tablets, and smartphones. Additionally, e-books often have lower production costs compared to print books, allowing for potentially higher profit margins. They also provide flexibility in pricing and promotional strategies, enabling authors to experiment with different pricing models and marketing tactics.

Formatting: Proper formatting is essential for e-books to ensure a professional appearance and compatibility with various e-reader devices. Use tools like Scrivener, Adobe InDesign, or Calibre to format your manuscript according to industry standards. Ensure that your e-book includes a clickable table of contents, properly formatted text, and high-quality images if applicable. Test your e-book on different devices and platforms to identify and address any formatting issues before publication.

Marketing: Effective marketing is crucial for the success of e-books. Utilise social media platforms, author websites, and online book communities to promote your e-book and engage with readers. Consider offering promotional discounts, participating in virtual book tours, and collaborating with book bloggers or influencers to increase visibility. Leverage online advertising options, such as Amazon Ads or Facebook Ads, to target specific audiences and drive sales. Building an email list and sending regular newsletters can also help maintain reader interest and generate sales.

Online Platforms:

As more literature moves online, the digital novel has become a fresh and exciting form of storytelling. Unlike traditional novels, digital novels often include multimedia elements like images, music, hyperlinks, and videos, making the reading experience more interactive and engaging. This multi-sensory approach allows readers to experience stories in a way that goes beyond just words on a page.

Platforms such as Wattpad and Radish have changed how writers share their work, offering them the chance to publish stories in a serial format. This means that writers can release chapters one at a time, allowing the story to unfold gradually. This method not only keeps readers engaged and eager for the next installment, but it also allows writers to receive real-time feedback from their audience, creating a sense of community between the author and the readers. Writers can adjust their stories based on reader reactions, making the process more collaborative.

Digital novels also blur the lines between traditional publishing and online writing communities. Writers have the freedom to experiment with different structures and formats, trying out new ways to tell stories. For instance, some digital novels might include interactive choices where readers can decide what happens next, while others may incorporate visuals or audio to set the tone or mood.

This new form of writing encourages episodic storytelling, where each part of the story builds on the last, similar to episodes in a TV series. This keeps readers coming back, eager to see how the plot unfolds. They also can be adapted to series and movies like the books from Wattpad *The Kissing Booth* Trilogy and *After* series were adapted into movies. Overall, digital novels open up new opportunities for creativity, giving writers the tools to create stories that are dynamic and immersive while reaching a global audience through online platforms.

Social media and Blogging: Building an online presence through social media and blogging can help you connect with readers and promote your work. Create and maintain profiles on platforms such as Twitter, Facebook, Instagram, and LinkedIn to share updates, engage with followers, and participate in literary conversations. Start a blog to share insights into your writing process, offer writing tips, and discuss relevant topics related to your genre. Engaging with readers and fellow writers through these platforms can help build a loyal following and generate interest in your work.

Digital Marketing: Digital marketing strategies play a crucial role in promoting e-books and online publications. Develop a comprehensive marketing plan that includes tactics such as search engine optimization (SEO), content marketing, and email campaigns. Use data analytics to track the effectiveness of your marketing efforts and make data-driven decisions. Explore opportunities for collaborations with other authors or organisations to expand your reach and increase visibility. Stay informed about emerging trends in digital marketing and adapt your strategies to leverage new opportunities for promoting your work.

Conclusion:

The world of creative writing has grown far beyond traditional methods, offering endless opportunities for writers to explore new ways of telling stories. From the short, impactful format of flash fiction to the visually engaging narratives in graphic novels, and the interactive nature of fanfiction, each new form gives writers a fresh avenue to connect with readers. These diverse formats allow writers to reach a broader audience, giving them the chance to express themselves in unique and creative ways.

As the digital world continues to evolve, so does the art of writing. The rise of blogs, podcasts, and interactive stories has changed how writers share their work. These platforms give writers the freedom to experiment with structure, style, and content, pushing the boundaries of what storytelling can be. Writers can now incorporate multimedia elements, like images and audio, to create a more immersive experience for readers. The internet has also opened up global access to new writers, enabling their work to reach audiences far beyond what was previously possible through traditional publishing routes.

Whether you're publishing an e-book, sharing a travel narrative, or crafting an audio story, the future of creative writing is full of unexplored potential. Innovation is everywhere, and as new technologies emerge, writers will have even more tools at their disposal to bring their stories to life. Getting yourself acquainted with these changes means opening yourself up to new ways of writing and connecting with others. The journey of publishing your work in this landscape which keeps on expanding is an exciting one.

Biopics of Writers That Will Make You Want to Write

Writers lead extraordinary lives—filled with passion, struggle, love, and relentless dedication to their craft. And sometimes, the best way to reignite your passion for writing is to witness the struggles, triumphs, and quiet moments of those who lived by the pen. Biopics about writers not only capture their literary legacy but also the human behind the words—their obsessions, heartbreaks, rebellion, discipline, and madness. The inspire us to keep writing, no matter the obstacles. If you are looking for the motivation, insight or just a great story, this list of powerful films that trace the lives of literary icons will reignite your creative spark. Whether rooted in fact or creative reinterpretation, each of these stories may help you pick up your pen again.

1. The Happy Prince (2018)

Story: This moving film explores the final years of Oscar Wilde's life—marked by exile, poverty, and deep reflection. Rupert Everett gives a haunting performance as Wilde, who grapples with the cost of his wit, love, and defiance of Victorian society.

Cast: Rupert Everett, Colin Firth, Colin Morgan.

2. Becoming Jane (2007)

Story: A romantic imagining of Jane Austen's early life and her love affair with Tom Lefroy, which may have inspired her novels. It reveals the tension between love and duty, and the limits placed on female writers of her time. Anne Hathaway delivers a captivating performance as a young Jane Austen, showing how her own romantic disappointments shaped classics like Pride and Prejudice.

Cast: Anne Hathaway, James McAvoy.

3. Bright Star (2009)

Story: This poetic visually stunning film centers on the tragic love affair between John Keats and Fanny Brawne. As Keats struggles with illness and critical rejection, the film captures his enduring passion for beauty, poetry, and love.

Cast: Ben Whishaw, Abbie Cornish.

4. The Man Who Invented Christmas (2017)

Story: A whimsical yet grounded portrayal of Charles Dickens as he writes *A Christmas Carol*. It shows how imagination, personal hardship, and financial strain shaped one of the most beloved stories of all time - perfect for writers facing deadlines!

Cast: Dan Stevens, Christopher Plummer.

5. Kill Your Darlings (2013)

Story: Based on the college days of Allen Ginsberg, this film explores his friendship with Lucien Carr and the early stirrings of the Beat Generation—set against a backdrop of obsession and murder. **Cast:** Daniel Radcliffe, Dane DeHaan.

6. Tolkien (2019)

Story: Chronicles the formative years of J.R.R. Tolkien—his friendships, love, and the trauma of war—which laid the groundwork for his legendary Middle-earth stories. A must-watch for fantasy writers!

Cast: Nicholas Hoult, Lily Collins.

7. A Quiet Passion (2016)

Story: A deeply introspective look at the life of poet Emily Dickinson. Cynthia Nixon's mesmerizing performance captures Dickinson's reclusive genius, fierce independence, her sharp wit, and unwavering resistance to societal norms.

Cast: Cynthia Nixon, Jennifer Ehle.

8. To Walk Invisible (2016)

Story: This BBC drama focuses on the Brontë sisters and their journey from obscurity to literary acclaim, showing how they defied 19th-century expectations to publish under male pseudonyms.

Cast: Finn Atkins, Charlie Murphy, Chloe Pirrie.

9. Sylvia (2003)

Story: This biopic traces the turbulent marriage of poets Sylvia Plath and Ted Hughes, and Plath's descent into despair and creative fury. **Cast:** Gwyneth Paltrow, Daniel Craig.

10. Miss Potter (2006)

Story: A charming film that follows the life of Beatrix Potter, author of *The Tale of Peter Rabbit*. It shows her as an artist, storyteller, and woman navigating a world that often dismissed her talent.

Cast: Renée Zellweger, Ewan McGregor.

11. Saving Mr. Banks (2013)

Story: While centered on Walt Disney's attempt to acquire the rights to *Mary Poppins*, the film equally focuses on author P.L. Travers and the trauma that shaped her writing.

Cast: Emma Thompson, Tom Hanks.

13. Kafka (1991)

Story: A surreal thriller merging Franz Kafka's real life with his fictional world. With noir tones and paranoia, the film explores themes of control, surveillance, and absurdity.

Cast: Jeremy Irons, Theresa Russell.

14. Rebel in the Rye (2017)

Story: A closer look at the life of reclusive writer J.D. Salinger and the creation of *The Catcher in the Rye*, exploring how war, love, and loss shaped his voice.

Cast: Nicholas Hoult, Kevin Spacey.

15. Finding Neverland (2004)

Story: A tender portrayal of J.M. Barrie's bond with the Llewelyn Davies family, which inspired *Peter Pan*. The film captures the interplay between loss and imagination.

Cast: Johnny Depp, Kate Winslet.

16. Pandaemonium (2000)

Story: Set in the Romantic period, it explores the friendship and rivalry between Samuel Taylor Coleridge and William Wordsworth, showing the tensions between vision, opium, and creativity.

Cast: Linus Roache, John Hannah.

These films remind us that writing is never easy—but it's always worth it. Whether you're battling self-doubt, financial struggles, or societal rejection, these writers' stories prove that perseverance leads to immortality through words. They help us understand how personal experiences shape art. The also provide a window into different eras and their influence on literature. These films don't just show writers writing. They reveal how life and literature mirror each other—messy, powerful, beautiful. You may not walk away with a new manuscript, but you'll likely feel less alone in your creative journey.